COACHING IN DEPTH

COACHING IN DEPTH

The Organizational Role Analysis Approach

Edited by

*John Newton, Susan Long,
and Burkard Sievers*

KARNAC
LONDON   NEW YORK

First published in 2006 by
H. Karnac (Books) Ltd.
6 Pembroke Buildings, London NW10 6RE

British Library Cataloguing in Publication Data

A C.I.P. for this book is available from the British Library

ISBN 1 85575 328 6

Edited, designed and produced by The Studio Publishing Services Ltd,
www.studiopublishingservicesuk.co.uk
e-mail: studio@publishingservicesuk.co.uk
Printed in Great Britain

10 9 8 7 6 5 4 3 2 1

www.karnacbooks.com

CONTENTS

John Bazalgette, Senior Consultant at The Grubb Institute, joined Bruce Reed from school teaching in 1966. He has consulted to leaders and executives in a variety of fields including global companies and small voluntary organizations, using the Institute's ORA method. He has worked extensively in the UK, France, Ireland, Spain and the Netherlands as well as the USA and Australia. Drawing on his experience in education he has written, lectured and broadcast about the ways in which organizational structures can support and further young people's growth and development in learning to take up adult roles in society.

Ullrich Beumer, Dipl. Päd.; Supervisor (DGSv); is Director of "inscape"—Institute for Psychoanalysis, Supervision und Organization Development, Coesfeld; Co-editor *Freie Assoziation*; Symposium Chair 2004 International Society for the Psychoanalytic Study of Organizations (ISPSO).

Hanna Biran, is a clinical psychologist and organizational consultant. She is a lecturer on Group Psychotherapy at the Tel-Aviv University, School of Medicine and works in private practice with individuals and groups. She is also a member of the Tel-Aviv Institute of Contemporary Psychoanalysis (TAICP), a member of the Israeli Institute of Group Analysis (IGA) and a member of ICS (Innovation and Change in Society).

Irving Borwick, MA (Chicago), PhD (Boston) is presently the Managing Director of Borwick International Inc., an international management consulting firm with offices in New York and Brussels. Borwick International specializes in bringing about change in large systems, with particular emphasis on strategic planning, corporate culture change, and organizational integration. Prior to this he held senior positions in the human resource field with Coca-Cola in Atlanta, Georgia, the International Telephone and Telegraph Company in Belgium, and Steinbergs Ltd in Canada. Before he entered the corporate world he lectured in English literature at McGill University, Montreal Canada. Dr Borwick has published numerous articles in journals and books.

Jane Chapman, BA, MBA, is a marketing and organizational consultant in Sydney, Australia and a member of the International Society for the Psychoanalytical Study of Organizations. Her work of recent years has had the aim of exploring the spaces between her two disciplines of marketing and organizational behaviour from a socio-analytic stance.

Laurence J. Gould, PhD is a Former Professor and Director, The Clinical Psychology Doctoral Program, The City University of New York, and Director of the Socio-Psychoanalytic Training Program, The Institute for Psychoanalytic Training and Research (IPTAR). He is the Co-Editor of *Organizational and Social Dynamics, An International Journal for the Integration of Psychoanalytic, Systemic and Group Relations Perspectives*, and is in the private practice of psychoanalysis and organizational consultation in New York City.

W. Gordon Lawrence, MA, Dr. rer. oec., is Managing Partner of Symbiont Technologies LLC, New York and a Director of Symbiont Ventures, London. He is a widely published innovator within the Group Relations tradition and is a former board member of the International Society for the Psychoanalytic Study of Organizations.

Susan Long, PhD, is Professor of Creative and Sustainable Organizations at Royal Melbourne Institute of Technology University, Australia. She is editor of *Socio-Analysis*, past President of the International Society for the Psychoanalytic Study of Organizations, and President of Group Relations Australia.

Rose Redding Mersky is an organizational development consultant and president of Redwood Executive Consulting, Inc., a firm that helps corporate executives and other leaders elevate morale, retain and attract valued employees, manage transitions, and enhance professional success. She is a past-President of the International Society for the Psychoanalytic Study of Organizations and its current Director of Professional Development. She is co-director of "Organizational Psychodynamics and Transformations", a professional development programme for managers, organizational consultants, supervisors, trainers, and psychoanalysts in Coesfeld, Germany. Her presentations and publications focus on the "intimacy" of consulting as a profession. She serves on the editorial board of the journal *Freie Assoziation*.

John Newton, PhD, is Associate Professor of Organization Dynamics at the Royal Melbourne Institute of Technology University, Melbourne, Australia, where he is the founding director of graduate programmes in Organization Dynamics. A member of the International Society for the Psychoanalytic Study of Organizations, his work as an educator, consultant, and action researcher is characterized by his interest in learning from experience.

Bruce Reed was Founder and President of The Grubb Institute of Behavioural Studies. An Australian, he first trained as an architect and was then ordained in the Church of England, studying theology in Sydney and at Cambridge. He became involved in the study of groups and organizations in the 1950s and worked with Ken Rice and Pierre Turquet in some of the earliest group relations conferences. Describing himself as an "organizational analyst", Bruce worked to develop a consistent framework of concepts and methods of study which would illuminate experience of life in organizations and communities. He generated a stream of original ideas about the interaction between person, system, context, and role, arising in particular from his work using ORA with leaders and executives in a wide range of organizations. The vast majority of these were presented in confidential consultancy reports, though some were expressed in lectures. His book, *The Dynamics of Religion*, published in 1978, has been a required text for theological students all over the world. The present paper is the last one he wrote before his death in November 2003.

Burkard Sievers, Dipl.-Soz., Professor of Organization Development, Bergische Universität Wuppertal; Co-editor *Freie Assoziation*; President (2005–2006), International Society for the Psychoanalytic Study of Organizations (ISPSO).

Introduction

John Newton, Susan Long, and Burkard Sievers

This book had its origins in conversations between the editors that were prompted by our links to the International Society for the Psychoanalytic Study of Organizations (ISPSO). In discussing the challenges and benefits of taking a psychoanalytic stance in our professional practice, whether in our teaching, research, or consultation services, we realized that increasingly we were using methods that were designed to enable individuals and work groups to find the courage, understanding, and authority to negotiate their work roles under conditions of persistent upheaval. A common thread we discovered in our professional histories was our involvement, initially at quite different times and places, in group relations conferences conducted in the tradition of the Learning for Leadership model developed at the Tavistock Institute of Human Relations, and first published by Rice (1965). We, like many other participants, had found our group relations experiences a profound exposure to the undercurrents of organizational life, within a setting and conceptual foundation that supported disciplined investigation of system psychodynamics, particularly as they impacted on task performance. Subsequently, each of us had incorporated and adapted this framework to our professional practice with individuals, groups, and organizations.

As our professional links expanded internationally, alongside the accelerating demand for management consultancy services including the current fashion for executive coaching, we decided it was time to bring attention and focus to the in-depth dimension of working with organizational role dynamics that had been stimulated by the group relations tradition. It was increasingly apparent that we, and others, had developed designs and methods that we referred to as Organizational Role Analysis (ORA), without there being any tight consistency among us about what we meant by the term. Among our colleagues there seemed to be a general acknowledgement of the influence of group relations methods, plus occasional references to two articles, long out of print. One article was authored by Bruce Reed (Reed, 1976), in which he outlined a method of individual consultancy being developed at the Grubb Institute of Behavioural Studies; the other by Gordon Lawrence (1979), which made a cogent argument for individuals to take up more responsibility for managing self in role, both as members of organizations and as citizens. Other published references were sparse and not easy to access.

Even though this book may be the first published collection of papers on the subject, it is not intended as a definitive statement on the practice of Organizational Role Analysis. As we approached potential contributors it soon became obvious to us that it would be pointless and self-defeating to try to specify any exact origins for the term, or to present Organizational Role Analysis as a uniform model. The late Eric Miller, long time Director of the Leicester Group Relations Conference (Miller, 1990) expressed similar sentiments in a personal communication:

"As I cast my mind back through the mists of time and clouds of pipe smoke, I remember Ken Rice in the mid-sixties first drawing attention to a form of role analysis within the design of group relations conferences. He offered some conceptualisation of it in his last publication (Rice, 1969). He and I began to use the term in our consultation work but many others have since developed their own approaches."

We found this last point to be much in evidence and quite consistent with the educational philosophy of the group relations tradition: one that encourages members of a conference to find their own authority for interpreting their experience and for applying their learning. As such, the chapters in this volume speak in distinctive voices, expressing various degrees of certitude, personal bias, conceptual development, and methodological formulation. What these authors offer in common is a disciplined stance in working collaboratively with their clients in order to help them disentangle the conscious and unconscious systemic forces impacting on their work roles. Collectively, what these contributors have shaped over time is an in-depth consulting/coaching approach that helps clients to work more effectively and humanely through their organizational roles. The emphasis is clearly on clarification of role within a system.

The book is divided in two sections. The first section comprises chapters by three of the people who shared in the gestation of the Organizational Role Analysis approach and who went on to develop unique formulations of the basic ideas; thus enriching the whole field. Irving Borwick's chapter begins the collection since he represents so strongly the end-user, the practising manager. Borwick has little time for the pieties of the various intellectual traditions he has investigated and which clearly inform his approach; what he has achieved through many years of in-house development is a design that puts the manager-in-role at the centre of a peer-driven inquiry into the systemic dimension of work problems and role performance. The clarity of his distinction between change of behaviour in role and change of personality will be welcomed by many who are dubious about the misguided and unrealistic claims of much of the "coaching" movement. In Chapter Two, Gordon Lawrence acknowledges Borwick for teaching him how to use role to think systemically, and for helping him to move away from his prior preoccupation with an individual focus; a move that he, and Biran in a later chapter, characterizes as the move from Oedipus to Sphinx. Lawrence very skilfully elucidates the necessary shift in psychoanalytic thinking that is necessary in order to move from the rightness/wrongness of the traditional psychoanalytic "interpretation" in a clinical setting, to the collaborative investigation invited by a "working hypothesis". His authoritative and lucid discussion of the continuing tension between the therapeutic use of psychoanalytic formulations and their systemic use for access to shared thinking about unconscious processes paves the way for the depth of understanding offered by ORA.

The third chapter in this section was commissioned from Bruce Reed, who died shortly before its completion and the manuscript was finalized by his longstanding colleague, John Bazalgette. Reed was the founding director of the Grubb Institute of Behavioural Studies, which has become well known for its development of concepts specific to its own practice of ORA as a form of consultancy in pastoral, commercial, and not-for-profit sectors. In contrast to Borwick, Reed and Bazalgette emphasize ORA as a form of one on one consultancy, best offered away from the day to day work context and conducted through a coherent framework for revealing the in-the-mind aspects of the client's role experience. The chapter charts a line of inquiry that assists the client to examine the dynamic process of finding, making, and taking up their organizational role. The focus is on the interaction between the psychological and sociological pressures on the person in role as the consultant assists the client to discern his/her organization-in-the-mind and test this against the aim of the system. As Bruce Reed's sadly unexpected last published paper it provides a rich compendium of his thinking about ORA.

The second section of the book provides an informative look at variations in the method and application of ORA from practitioners in different parts of the world. Burkard Sievers and Ullrich Beumer provide an artful exposition of Kleinian theory in considering how the work organization becomes an object in the inner world of a client, entangled with the authority structures derived from her childhood experience and made accessible through the use of work drawings within the ORA process. The admissibility of the client's broader mission in life is made possible through a firm focus on the connection between the inner and outer worlds of her organizational role experience. Next, Hanni Biran picks up Bion's metaphor of "binocular vision", differentiating the focus of analysis between Oedipus and Sphinx, the narcissistic and the socialistic, the individual and the organizational. With a telling reference to the cultural narcissism that bedevils the Israeli–Palestinian context within which she lives and works, Biran offers a hopeful case study that illustrates how the use of ORA, as part of a larger intervention within an Israeli school sector, helped to release clinical

psychologists from the constraints of their individualized, therapeutic frame in order to consider their work with at-risk, immigrant
students as a mirror to the systemic pressures within the school sector. The effect of this ORA work on encouraging the psychologists
to examine their role in relation to other roles within the educational system is a wonderful illustration of Lawrence's earlier argument for the capacity of ORA to refract the social in the individual's
experience.

In Chapter Six, Long, Newton, and Chapman report their
serendipitous adaptation of the one on one ORA method to create a
process of "role dialogue" between role holders in a prison system
whose functions had become unwittingly and progressively disconnected. This new design, in which "role" was supported to speak to
"role" (within a system that was plagued by interpersonal gossip
and informal power structures), was part of a long-term action
research project around the introduction of a new, "case management" task that required many different role holders to re-construe
the relatedness of their roles in pursuit of the shared organizational
task. The following chapter, by Rose Redding Mersky, illustrates
another departure from common practice with her honest and
thoughtful reflection on the advisability of conducting an ORA by
telephone. Mersky recounts in some detail her lengthy consultation
to a corporate client who preferred not to meet face to face. Denied
the usual visual and contextual clues, Mersky developed a disciplined process of note taking and professional supervision to work
with the latent dynamics of a client who "preferred not to be seen"
while she struggled with the politics of an executive career. Mersky
concludes that ORA by telephone may not be optimal but it can
work, and may have to, as senior managers are less willing and able
to commit the time for regular, face to face appointments.

Susan Long, in Chapter Eight, describes another methodological
innovation with her use of "role biography" as a part of the ORA
process. Role biography refers to the pattern of role taking that the
client may have developed across their life; beginning in the family,
then through adolescent incursions into the world of work, and
right up to the present. The pattern of role biography may be con-
trasted with the history of the client's work role within its organizational system, and may be used to help the client discern her/his
predisposition for role taking that they bring to their current work

role experience. In the following chapter, Laurence Gould similarly highlights a belatedly obvious yet neglected aspect of the client's role experience by examining it as an aspect of life stage. Using his considerable command of life cycle theory, Gould argues persuasively that at different stages of a client's life, his/her work role will be a vehicle for the playing out of tensions characteristic of that stage of life. His case example poignantly illustrates how a senior client's dilemma between a continuing executive position and a return to line management is as much about the client's feelings to do with mortality, legacy, and reparation as it is about what would be best for the firm. Significantly, it is the consultant's own access to "senior-hood" that allows such feelings to be presented in the consultancy and to be worked with.

The final chapter in the volume documents John Newton's achievement in adapting the principles of Organizational Role Analysis to a successful form of management education within a graduate university programme. His design confronts the prevailing orthodoxy of MBA-style learning *about* management by challenging and supporting students to learn through direct experience the systemic mind-set and emotional capacities necessary for managing oneself in role.

These ten chapters, considered as a whole, present a varied and lively introduction to the intellectual origins and contemporary practice of Organizational Role Analysis. They do so without closing off possibilities for further development and, hopefully, these contributions will encourage a new generation of "coaches" to utilize ORA's professional discipline and conceptual focus to work in sufficient depth with their clients to make a worthwhile difference to their role performance, their organizations and society. The book concludes with some brief comments about future directions.

These contributions are accompanied by an extensive bibliography, compiled by Burkard Sievers with the assistance of members of ISPSO.

PART I
ORGANIZATIONAL ROLE ANALYSIS:
FROM THERE TO HERE

CHAPTER ONE

Organizational Role Analysis: managing strategic change in business settings

Irving Borwick

T his quest began forty years ago in my role as a teacher when I was lecturing on English Literature at McGill University. Twenty years later I developed the first systemic programme, the *Group Strategy and Action Program*® and as part of that development, the Organizational Role Analysis was developed.

The quest

I sought to develop a programme and a process that ensures participants will transform ideas into action. From my earliest days as a teacher I have been confronted with students and managers who avow their undying commitment to new ideas. However, their behaviour belies every syllable they utter. It fascinates me that so many can be committed to so much and do so little about it. My single-minded search has been to bridge what I call the "gap" between idea and action (Figure 1).

Individuals walk away from speeches, programmes, learning experiences of all kinds, dedicated and emotionally committed to a new idea or concept they have learned. Yet, they do not change their behaviour one iota—and they are still dedicated to the change.

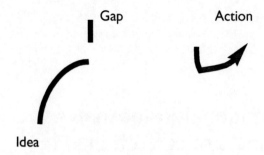

Figure 1. The gap between idea and action.

The search for the paradigm of change that would transform ideas into actions took me through the Group Dynamics Movement, the T-Group Movement, Tavistock Group Relations Conferences, The Milan Family Therapy Centre, and the Systems movement.

Group Dynamics

Group Dynamics provided tools and techniques for managing group processes. To that degree it was very helpful and insightful. However, in my experience, it has little impact in changing ideas into action.

The Group Dynamics strategy is to provide an "ah-ha" experience. It assumes that insight leads to action. The result is that most group dynamics programs are a series of unrelated exercises or role-plays, each of which provides some insight. If you add them up they are supposed to lead to understanding and that is supposed to lead to change.

Tavistock Institute of Human Relations

Next came the Tavistock Group Relations process, which was brilliant and quite effective, but so punitive and brutal in its impact that it created as many negative reactions as positive experiences. And even the positive experiences were positive upon reflection, not while being experienced. Consequently, I attempted to integrate the anaemic blandness of Group Dynamics with the rough treatment of the Tavistock Group Relations approach to create a process that would achieve the impact of the Tavistock method without the accompanying pain. Pierre Turquet (Director of the annual Tavistock Group Relations Conference before his early death) and I once ran such a programme together. However, it was not so much an integrated programme as two parallel tracks. He did his thing and I did mine.

Systems Thinking

The next development occurred when I became acquainted with the clinical applications of Systems Thinking. My wife, Bella Borwick, then Chairman of the Family Therapy Department at the University of Louvain, invited Luigi Boscolo and Gianfranco Cecchin of the Milan Family Therapy Centre to Brussels for a week to demonstrate their newly developed systemic techniques. I joined this group, although I am not a therapist.

Milan Family Therapy Institute

For a week I sat and marvelled at the brilliance of these two men. With tapes, stories, anecdotes, and live cases they demonstrated their systemic theory and techniques. They had cured anorexics, which had never been achieved until then; they cured catatonic patients in four or five months, they wrought marvellous changes in a brief time without huge conflicts. I was overwhelmed. If they could achieve such results with pathological patients, imagine what could be achieved in a business environment with normal, healthy managers.

Before they left Brussels I hired them to work with me for a year, two days a month, to develop their techniques for managers at ITT Europe, where I was the Director of Organization Development. For ten months we struggled and finally had to quit. Managers were calling me up and asking if I was trying to ruin their lives. What worked so well with families was a disaster with managers.

Permanent role versus temporary role

After some reflection, I began to develop a hypothesis. The techniques of the Milan Family Therapy Centre were powerful interventions that exploded and exposed the family system. No one in the family was threatened by such powerful interventions because it is impossible to lose your role in the family. You retain your role as mother, father, brother, sister, son, or daughter all your life. You may be the last remaining member of your family, but you will still retain these roles; they are permanent. On the other hand, your role in a business organization is always temporary. You can hold the title of Director for fifty years, but when you retire or leave the company you lose the company role and all the benefits that go with it. I hypothesized that the therapeutic interventions of the Milan approach threatened managers at work in a way they never threatened family members in the clinic. The managers felt in danger of losing their roles in the work system if they exposed that system. They feared losing their jobs and with it their livelihood, their economic security, and their families.

I made the decision then to develop a process equal to that developed by the Milan Family Therapy Group, based upon the same systemic theories and capable of achieving the same powerful results, swiftly, and without trauma or turbulence to the system. The goal was to create a programme and a process that would move people from ideas to action, that would, finally, change behaviour. The MODEL was in sight.

The search for the paradigm continues

For the next four and a half years I experimented with systemic theory to create a systemic programme. I worked with numerous colleagues during these years, but primarily three were involved: Gordon Lawrence (see Chapter Two), Bruce Reed (see Chapter Three), and Siggy Hirsch. Each supported the effort and contributed to the unfolding meaning and understanding of our experience. Gordon's insights were particularly helpful. The first successful programme was the Group Strategy and Action Program®, which became a short circuit to change as if it was an integrated circuit compared to the vacuum tube technology that I had been using. What previously had taken years to change could be done in months or even weeks. As part of the development of the Group Strategy and Action Program®, the Organizational Role Analysis was developed.

The role of role

The key issue in systemic change is to change the role and not the person or the organization. I was sensitized to roles because of my work with representatives of the Milan Institute. I began to look at the role and not the person. The abstract notion of systems became more concrete when I could think of people in their roles and not about their characters.

Role is the link between the individual and the organization. I am linked to my company by my role. If I lose the role I lose my connection to the organization. I am out of the system. The organization defines the role and hires someone to fill the role. The company needs a salesman, or an engineer, or a production manager. It does not necessarily need Sam or Joe, Ann or Louise. As Figure 2 emphasizes, a clear distinction can be made between a focus on "role" and a focus on the individual's character.

Role is a pivotal factor in managing change. Prior to this we had focused on the individual or the organization. Often we use both approaches: the organizational followed by the individual. My new conception was of role connecting the individual to the organizational system, as depicted in Figure 3.

I now realized that it was the role that had to change, not the person. And I immediately thought of my old boss. Many years ago I worked for a manager who was authoritarian, given to much screaming and shouting. One day, after attending a programme, he learned that one role of a manager is to listen. He redefined his role

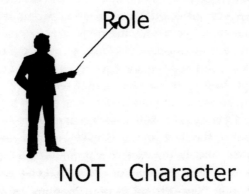

Figure 2.   Focus on role, not on an individual's character

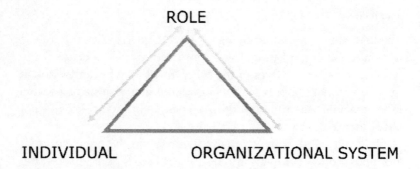

ROLE

INDIVIDUAL   ORGANIZATIONAL SYSTEM

Figure 3.   The role–individual–organizational system triangle.

as a manager as one who also listens. He did not change his personality. At the next management meeting, after his traditional screams and shouts, he explained that he was now going to listen. He then gave the command, "Talk, I'm listening." And he did listen. He had changed his understanding of his role—and consequently his behaviour—but not his personality.

"Change without change"

To change the role yet not change the person is the challenge of what I call "Change without change". We do it every day; change our role, but not our personality. Every time we change role we also change behaviour. In the office you may be commanding and decisive, but as a spouse you may be uncertain and diffident. You may be an obedient employee, but a domineering parent. It all depends how you understand your role, the rules of your system, and the relations you have established. One may think of the organization as a network of roles and relations governed by a set of rules, and various people take up those roles as they see them.

Changing the role can theoretically bring almost instant change in behaviour. Of course, the key to such change is the acceptance by the individual of the new role. It is even better if the individual creates the new role. In the case of a promotion, the job changes dramatically and the expectation for a changed behaviour is universal. But changing your role is not easy. Systems are like gravity; they have a weight and power that extends everywhere and is seen nowhere. The weight of your experience in your role and the power of others' expectations can act as cement in maintaining the status quo. The strongest rationale for not changing one's role is not knowing what one should do in one's new role.

Organizational Role Analysis (ORA)

The management of change involves three major factors: The individual, the role, and the system. As I said above, Role connects the Individual to the System. As part of the *Group Strategy and Action Program*® process we created three major interventions: one intervention to deal with the individual (the Mapping Exercise), one to deal with the role (The Organizational Role Analysis), and the third to deal with the system (The Systems Analysis).

The Mapping Exercise introduces new information into the system. For the first time, for most people, the interior organization of their mental world is externalized so they can look at it on a piece of paper. They can see on this piece of paper what they were feeling or thinking in their head. For the first time, often, they can examine the "soft" data, i.e., feelings, intuition, etc., as specific, moveable, and manipulative data. They can and do begin to take what appear to be fixed ideas and treat them as temporary arrangements that can be altered.

The Organizational Role Analysis redefines the individual's role in the system. Building upon the unfreezing of the internal map of the individual, the ORA makes it possible for the individual to explore, with the help of others, the current way in which the role is understood and managed by the organization but implemented by the manager in the role. The individual becomes an observer of herself; she can look at herself from outside the box.

The Systems Analysis provides the opportunity for the entire system to examine its relations. This is done collectively and in subsystems to visibly and conceptually understand what makes the system function the way it does. It is both an intervention and an analysis of the system.

This chapter concentrates on the ORA, which has its roots in many places. Let me try to pull together, after many years, some of the strands that went into the development of the ORA.

Hypothesis development

Sometime in the mid 1970s my wife, Bella Borwick, invited Harry Aponte from Philadelphia to work with her in Brussels. As part of the invitation, I agreed to utilize him to consult to me in ITT. This was partially to defray expenses for the university and also because I was always interested in new ideas. Aponte focused heavily on the use of hypotheses. His argument, which I found very persuasive, was that hypotheses are conjectures, guesses, hunches, but they are not facts. Unlike opinions, which are fixed and tend to induce defensive responses if the opinion is challenged, hypotheses are ephemeral. They may be accurate, but are probably not. You need to constantly update, improve, or throw them away and create new ones. As I like to say, you never marry a hypothesis, you only flirt with it.

Aponte worked with one of our managers for a day and was very helpful in bringing about a change. But what was important for me was the concept of hypothesis as a means of introducing ideas without creating conflict and of treating information as temporary not permanent. Truth exists, but we can only approximate it. Through constant redefining of our hypotheses we can get closer and closer to the truth, but we can never own it. This allows us to develop many ideas and not to get fixed or blocked into defending them. And even when we discover an hypothesis that appears to be accurate, to be true, it does not take long to discover that there are even deeper hypotheses that are more accurate. In other words, hypothesis development is a truly scientific methodology that aids us in pursuing knowledge and understanding, not in some distant theoretical way, but in a gut-wrenching, observational way, without inducing anger, conflict, strife, or resistance.

The ORA is structured around the development of hypotheses, not opinions. From beginning to end the ORA requires one to ask questions and to provide a hypothesis for each question. All discussion is around hypotheses; and all answers are conjectures or hypotheses. At no time does one try to pin "truth" down. One is always in a state of getting closer and closer to the "truth" but never arriving. This means that every hypothesis must be tested, challenged, and examined and newer, better, more accurate hypotheses developed.

Appearance versus "reality"

It became clear, as we worked within the organization, that almost every problem brought to us was not the "real" problem. In other words, there was clearly something else going on. It became a rule that whatever the client identified as the problem, that was probably not the problem. It does not mean the client is wrong, or lying, or misleading us. It means that there are other things in addition to what he or she is telling us.

If a manager blames his employees for being lazy and that is the reason for their low productivity, we assume that he certainly believes this. Within his understanding of *his role*, it might well be a reasonable hypothesis. However, if we go deeper we are likely to discover that the overt laziness is directly related to a systemic rule and relation that in turn is directly related to the manager's understanding of his role.

The challenge is to help the manager discover the underlying nature of the system and not to explain it to him or advise him. This is based upon the discovery principle.

The discovery principle

In the late 1950s and early 1960s, before the advent of personal computers, Programmed Instruction was a hot item. Today, no one has heard of it. Programmed Instruction is a process for programming data in such a manner that the reader is forced to deduce the answer from the information provided. She has to discover the answer. That, at least, is one of the major tenets of the tool.

Information is provided, followed by a question of some kind. The answer to the question can only be *discovered* by deducing it from the information provided. One has to discover the answer for oneself. It is never provided directly. It seems that when one discovers something for oneself, one retains it. When someone tells you the answer you tend to remember it for a limited amount of time, if at all.

Research done by the Bell Telephone Company back in the 1950s demonstrated that students taught by Programmed Instruction outperformed, in every case, students taught by their best lecturers. It was an extraordinary piece of research and the results were lopsided in supporting the effectiveness of Programmed Instruction in learning. It is a sad fact that Programmed Instruction has all but disappeared. However, the discovery principle is no less effective in helping managers to learn. Moreover, the discovery principle was reinforced by the Tavistock methodology, which tended to leave the burden for learning to the individual. Each individual was accountable for his or her own discovery about how they exercised power and authority. In the Tavistock approach, minimal support or help is given the individual. The discovery principle and the final evolution of the Organizational Role Analysis was and is much more supportive.

Systems Thinking and Organizational Role Analysis

Organizational Role Analysis was developed through trial and error. At this point in time there is no possibility of laying out the step by step development. The concepts described above played a significant role in this development. The most significant influence, however, is systems thinking.

Systems Thinking is holistic. A system is a frame within which behaviour is contained. Psychology examines behaviour; whereas systems thinking examines the containing frame and how the container influences what is contained. However, it does not examine what is contained. For example, your role is the frame and your personality is contained within that frame. In psychological terms, getting angry could be the results of some early trauma or developed trait. It is a part of your character or make-up. In system terms, getting angry might be the assigned task of that role as understood by the person occupying the role. If I am the boss and I understand the role in hierarchical terms, then I might imagine that I have the right and the responsibility to become angry if you do not follow my orders.

This is easiest seen when a worker is promoted to the role of supervisor. As a worker, it is not his business as to who is working and who is idling. As a supervisor it is his responsibility. A perfectly nice fellow can turn into a dictator when promoted to the role of supervisor. Not because he is a nasty fellow, but because he believes that is his role. The same is true of parents. A perfectly reasonable woman, when she becomes a parent, believes that she is responsible for the moral character and disciplining of the child. She can inflict punishment of a rather nasty kind, believing that is her job, her role, her responsibility.

Organizational Role Analysis allows the individual to examine her behaviour as it relates to the role and not to her person. It does this at different levels of meaning.

Organizational Role Analysis and Levels of Meaning

An Organizational Role Analysis helps an individual to uncover the several layers of meaning they use to define the role. The objective of the role analysis is not to solve the problem, but to understand how we take up our roles in the system. The real problem is that managers often solve the problems they know how to solve, not the problems they actually have. Finding solutions is *not* the most difficult task; it is knowing the difference between a symptom and a problem. Our task is to understand the problem and go beyond the symptom.

The Pirandello effect: five levels of meaning

The Pirandello effect, named after the Italian playwright, describes five levels of meaning, or views of reality. The Pirandello effect works simultaneously at five different levels, as depicted in Figure 4.

The first Pirandello effect is the *symptom*. A problem or issue is presented. We call this the symptom. We can see it or describe it. It is a common enough phenomenon.

The second Pirandello effect is the *root meaning* and connects symptoms or objects. The root system is underground, as the term suggests, and is not readily apparent. When uncovered it makes apparent the connections between the parts of the system. It is the pattern that connects one thing to another.

The third Pirandello effect connects root systems into an *area meaning*. An area meaning contains and unites the pattern that connects one piece of behaviour to another. An area meaning tends to offer alternative explanations for surface behaviours.

The area meanings unite into what we might call the *macrosystem* that connects a number of area systems.

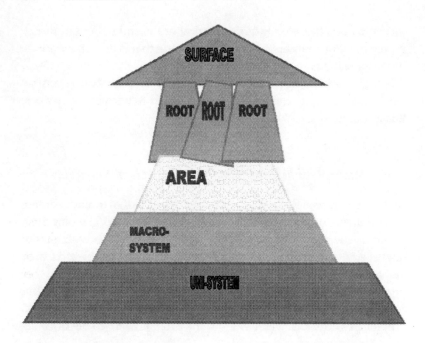

Figure 4.   Pirandello with five tiers.

And last, the assembly of all the macrosystems combine into a *unisystem*. This connects all macrosystems and looks at the entire universe in its largest perspective.

Every ORA is designed with the hope of uncovering the root system and the area system. On occasions one is able to uncover the macrosystems. The guiding principle is to try to deal with three levels of effect: symptom, root and area, whatever the issue you are confronting.

Organizational Role Analysis: Example

Let us look at a real role analysis. A customs agent tells the following story. She manages all customs declarations that go through customs on behalf of the XYZ Company, an overnight delivery service in Europe. If the XYZ Company transporters follow the rules, then most, if not all, deliveries will go through customs without problems.

However, she is constantly confronted with violations of customs' rules by the company transporters. And no matter how much she complains or attempts to apply pressure to get them to follow the simple rules, they continue to violate the rules daily. Why?

The reason is simple. The company prides itself on its basic service of delivering overnight, on time. To do this requires that documents and parcels be picked up as late as possible to accommodate the customer. On the other hand, it is crucial to see that these late pick-ups get on the planes that leave each evening. Consequently, from the point of view of the transporters who perform the basic service of the company for the customer, getting it there on time is the most important thing. Frequently, they have to push a document or a parcel, or many of them, on to a plane before the paperwork has been completed. They may complete it partially or not at all. Whatever it takes to get it on the plane and into the other country on time is worthwhile, from their perspective. The fact that it may be returned, or may never get through customs, or be held up for days is immaterial to the transporters. They got it there on time. The problem of delivering it once it arrives in the other country is not their problem. Sure, they did not follow the exact procedures. But they did get it to the destination country on time.

Organizationally, there is no connection between the transporters and the company customs agent. They each work for different bosses. The transporters' boss can boast that his department delivers on time at 98 or 99%. Returns are not counted in the statistics for on-time performance.

The root meaning

The customs agent is totally discouraged. What can she do to influence the situation so that the transporters will follow the elementary customs rules? At the root level, the customs agent and the transporter are intimately connected. The customs agent makes it possible for the transporters to continue to violate the customs rules. She works very hard to ensure that the documents and parcels get through customs. And they do, more or less. The number of actual returns never gets so large that it causes a problem.

A different situation would exist if the customs agent did not do her job so well and many more parcels and documents were returned. Transporters would be confronted with the problem. As it now stands, they do not have to face the results of their failure to follow procedure. In fact, they are rewarded for breaking the rules. They achieve high, on-time results.

The company transporters are happy but the customs agent is not. The customs agent sees herself as the "good one", doing the right thing, saving the company, and making the system work. She also sees the transporters as the "bad ones", who violate the rules, create customs problems, create unnecessary costs, delay delivery of goods, and sometimes actually impede the working of the whole system.

From the point of view of the *customs agent*, it is the company transporters who need to change, not the customs agent. But they won't. The customs agent has asked, pleaded, threatened, begged, and argued, but to no avail.

The *agent and the transporters* now have a contract, so to speak. The company transporters will violate the customs rules to get the goods to the destination on time. The customs agent will repair the violations, under duress. The company transporters will see themselves as the good ones because they achieve their company goal: to get the goods to the destination on time. The customs agent will see herself as the good one, because, in spite of all the bad things done by the transporters she continues to solve the problems over and over, thus protecting and saving the company. Neither will change. The system is in perfect balance and working well. Except the customs agent is dreadfully unhappy.

The area system

The ORA reveals the pattern that connects. Examination of the role, not the person, swiftly allows us to explore a significant issue. What is the described role played by the customs agent in this situation? The *defined* role of the customs agent is to facilitate the entry of goods across boundaries. The described role of the customs agent as performed and described above is to fight fires created by transport violators.

Consequently, the *systemic* role of the customs agent is to prevent change from occurring and to preserve the current transit processes. As long as the custom agent repairs the violations of the company transporters, they do not have to change. Therefore, the customs agent's actual systemic role is to ensure a non-change system.

The customs agent and the company transporter each feel that they are the good guys. They are doing what is right to protect the company. Each feels the other is the problem. If the customs agent would just do her job instead of complaining then everything would be all right. After all, what is the role of the customs agent if not to deal with missing or bad data?

The customs agent feels that if the transporters would just do the simple task of supplying the data, which they have available to them, then thousands of documents and parcels that are now held up would get through customs without any problem and would be delivered on time. It is only by sheer grit and determination and long hours that the customs agent is able to partially resolve the problems.

THE ROLES OF THE COMPANY TRANSPORTER

SURFACE: Defined role: deliver on time;
ROOT: Described role: do whatever it takes to satisfy customer and to deliver on time;
AREA: Systemic role: mobilize customs agent to ensure on time delivery.

THE ROLES OF THE CUSTOMS AGENT

SURFACE: Defined role: facilitate goods entry across boundary;
ROOT: Described role: to fight fires;
AREA   Systemic role: prevent change from occurring; maintain the current system.

The macrosystem

The macrosystem is the XYZ Company and all similar delivery types of services. The marketing strategy of XYZ is on time delivery, guaranteed. The marketing strategy of competitors varies from low cost, longer-term delivery to overnight, on time delivery.

The Customs department of the XYZ Company supports the work of the customs agent to bring the company transporters into line. But the XYZ Company, separating the function of delivery and customs control in two departments with no organizational bridge except at the very top of the organization, supports the pattern of isolation and separation. There is no organizational structure designed to connect the two departments or facilitate integrated action. By maintaining the separation of the two departments, the XYZ organization ensures a non-change strategy with regard to this issue and supports the company transporters on time goals.

In other words, the XYZ Company has designed a system that ensures achievement of its primary task: to deliver on time.

One may contrast this strategy with other delivery services and develop some hypotheses as to the nature of world-wide delivery services.

The unisystem

The unisystem is the marketplace, which could be the country or the global market. In either case, the issue is related directly to how business designs its structures to support its goals. Do businesses in general design and develop their organizations in such a way as to create non-change strategies in support of their primary goals, or do they develop strategies that facilitate goal achievement without handicapping one subsystem to ensure the success of another?

Before examining the ORA process, I would like to emphasize that the exploration revolves around the first three levels described above: surface, root, and area. It does not go to the deepest levels of macrosystems and unisystem.

Organizational Role Analysis: structure and process

Psychology focuses upon the individual, while systems focus upon the relations and rules governing roles. Psychology tends to segregate the individual, while systems thinking integrates. Character or personalities are the touchstones of psychology; role rules and relations are the connecting points of systems. In the end, psychology attempts to deal with groups and organizations as the sum total of many personalities. It often attempts to create the group in the image of the individual. Thus, we hear of group personality or character. By contrast, a system is any set of relations with a boundary, having rules developed over time. And the connecting factor is role. Role is the fundamental connecting construct. The system defines the roles and the individuals take up the roles, refining and defining the role further. The interplay between the individual and the system to define role, at the same time co-defines the system. System is, by definition, an integrating construct, while psychology is a differentiating construct. Role connects the individual to the system and the system to the individual. This fundamental fact determines the nature of relations within the system. We need to contrast this with the psychological point of view that connects the individual to the group by character or personality. The implications are enormous.[1]

Consider some differences as outlined below.

PSYCHOLOGY	SYSTEMS
1 Behaviour is a function of character or personality	1 Behaviour is a function of role definition and relation
2 Personality or character formed by nature and nurture	2 Role defined by system and individual interaction
3 Actions grounded in character	3 Actions grounded in systems rules and relations
4 Change in behaviour requires personality/character change	4 Change in behaviour requires redefining role, rules and relations.
5 Change is difficult and long term	5 Change is challenging, but swift and effective.

Given these assumptions, the Organizational Role Analysis is designed to examine a role in terms of rules and relations, and to avoid, wherever possible, character or personality analysis. Hence some important specifications govern its effectiveness.

Specifications for the ORA

- ORA is fundamentally a group process (or more accurately, a system process) and not a one-on-one process. Yet it is certainly adaptable to one-on-one and from the articles that follow, it might appear that it is the primary methodology. When adapted to a psychological or psychiatric mode, then it is clearly the most appropriate methodology. As a systemic tool, the ORA is not one-on-one, but a small system process.

- The underlying strategy in every systemic consultation is that the burden of the process lies with the individual presenter, not with the consultant. The ORA is a voluntary process. The Presenter volunteers to present and the members who join the ORA process volunteer to join that specific group. The volunteer Presenter knows beforehand that the ORA will be conducted in a small group, but she or he does not know who will be in the group. When the members of the Group are also members of the organization, the learning for both the volunteer and the group is significantly enhanced.

- The act of volunteering places the responsibility for the learning on the volunteer. This is important, because consultants often feel responsible to help the client and to solve the problem. This impedes the learning process by shifting the responsibility from the shoulders of the client to that of the consultant. Moreover, participants often join a process or programme with the assumption that they have done their job by coming to the programme, now it is up to the consultant or teacher to teach. They are willing to learn, but not to take responsibility for the learning. I suspect that one of the most serious barriers to learning is the teacher or consultant who assumes so much responsibility for the student that the student never has to assume any responsibility.

- The ORA is not an exercise nor a role-play. The volunteer needs to identify a current issue or problem, which is unresolved, in which she or he has a role responsibility, which can be a small, medium, or large issue, the outcome of which is important to the volunteer.

- The fact that the ORA is done in a group setting and not isolated is important. It means that a subset of the system is already participating in the re-examination of the role. To place the role under scrutiny is to place the system under the same scrutiny. If the role is connected to the system, there is no way you can look at the role without looking at the system. This becomes apparent very quickly.

- The ORA process is designed to ensure full examination of the issue, while containing and regulating the process to prevent any turbulence, i.e., emotional eruptions. On many occasions we have had an ORA Presenter (volunteer) reviewing a conflicted relation with a boss, colleague, or subordinate with that individual in the room, participating in the process. On no occasion in twenty years has there been a conflict or blow-up.
- Surface, symptom–root–area effects: one might say that identification of the issue is a surface factor. The operating assumption is that this is a symptom, probably not the actual issue. Identification of the underlying systemic issue is the root issue. The sum of the issues identified within a programme or a process is the system talking directly to us. If we do nine role analyses within a programme, we have nine issues. If we can identify the pattern that connects these nine issues, we now have a solid hypothesis about the system as a whole.

Given these specifications, a model ORA is divided into four basic parts:

Step 1: Problem presentation
Step 2: Systemic analysis
Step 3: System reflection
Step 4: Individual reflection

Step 1

The ORA is deceptively simple. It opens with the volunteer presenting and explaining the issue from her perspective and providing an organizational chart showing the managers whom she experiences as part of the problem.

Step 2

The role of the participant managers who have joined this ORA is now explained. They are asked to take up the role of "consultant" to the Presenter. The "consultants" are encouraged to ask questions. *There is only one rule.* For each question asked they must also provide a hypothesis. The hypothesis is their conjecture, guess, hunch, feeling, intuition, as to what the answer is. No question will be answered without the hypothesis to support it. This is an iron-clad rule. For every question asked there must be an hypothesis.

Once an answer is given, the consultants may not quarrel with it. They may believe it or not. If they think the answer is not correct, they may not quarrel with the Presenter. The only resort is to ask more and better questions.

Step 3

After questioning for a while, and when it seems appropriate, a time-out is called. The group then discusses the hypotheses they have developed based upon the questions that have been asked and answered. The Presenter may not participate in this discussion, but may listen only.

One may return to step two and then step three, circulating between them until one finally reaches a set of hypotheses that one believes are more or less close to explaining the nature of the role as it is lived. Having reached this point, one moves on to *step four.*

Step 4

The Presenter is asked for her reaction to the set of hypotheses and her experience of the Organizational Role Analysis. The Presenter has the last word, and the session is closed.

The entire ORA is scheduled usually to last one and a half hours.

Commentary and practical hints

Goal of the Organizational Role Analysis

The goal of the ORA is not to solve the problem; it is to identify what the real issue is. In the example above the obvious problem, as presented by the custom agent, is that the transport managers would not do their job. They did not fill out the required customs papers.

It is clear that if you know the real problem, you can find three or more solutions almost immediately. Finding solutions is easy. We can imagine any number of approaches for getting the transporters to fill out the customs papers. But filling out papers is not the problem. It is the presenting problem, a symptom. If we work at resolving the presenting problem then the underlying, systemic issue is neglected.

Identifying the issue is not easy. That is why so many solutions do not work. Rather than identify the real issue, managers frequently assume what the problem is and develop solutions to solve that problem, a problem they know how to solve, but not the problem they have.

Presenting the issue

What the Presenter presents is seldom the real issue. It is most often a symptom. The ORA "consultants" are asked not to help the Presenter with information as they present, since what a Presenter "forgets" to include is also information. Moreover, most Presenters will not present the entire picture. Somebody or something is frequently left out. One of the most common inaccuracies is to present two levels of management. To understand what is happening in a system, it is almost always necessary to see three levels of organization, as illustrated in Figure 5: the level above and the level below. In every situation I am contained by a system and I contain systems. All too often managers present two levels, believing the third level is not involved.

The role of the hypothesis

I am usually relaxed about following rules too closely. A little flexibility always seems preferable. Over time, however, I learned that it is necessary to insist upon the question first and the hypothesis second, and to insist on a hypothesis for every question, without exception. Why?

Because the offering of an hypothesis affects the Presenter and the consultants in a number of different ways. Without an hypothesis

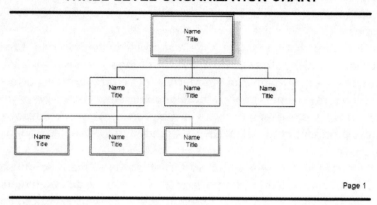

Figure 4. Three level organization chart.

the question is no longer a conjecture, it is a kind of "truth". At the very least it is a position. Whatever we say has the burden of being seen as some kind of fact or position that has to be defended or challenged. This leads to conflict, argument, and disagreement. There can be little understanding when we are defending or attacking ideas. We become victims of our positions, defenders of our truth, and assailants of the other's ideas. A hypothesis is a flimsy. For sure, it is never totally accurate. We need to replace hypotheses constantly, refine them, improve them, and create new ones to get closer and closer to some kind of truth. We never reach the truth, but we can get closer to it.

With hypotheses we are always in a state of becoming and never in a state of arrival. We are open for new ideas and never closed to another hypothesis. This is why hypotheses are so important and cannot be ignored. The hypothesis diminishes the question and levels the playing field. It permits the Presenter and the consultant–questioner to be on the same side, looking for understanding; not adversaries in a win–lose battle.

The need to give advice

We all seem to need to give advice. "Don't you think that if you did such and such . . ." is a standard opening question for advice givers. It is not really a question, but advice disguised as a question, followed by the implicit hypothesis that I am correct and that is what you need to do.

The problem is that we do not know what the problem is. Managers constantly jump to the conclusion that they know the problem and have an answer. The problem is that they have answers for the problems they know how to solve, not the problems they actually have. One of the key issues in a role analysis is to avoid solution-giving and to pursue understanding. When you seek beyond the obvious and attempt to plumb the depths of meaning to get to the root effects and the area effects underlying a problem, you are in danger of frightening the consultants. The Presenter already knows that she has undertaken a risk in exploring what is going on in her organization. Presenters are usually quite sanguine about the process. But the consultants usually assume that they are outside the problem, and quickly discover, if they are part of the organization, that they are, or may be, part of the situation. They can run, but they cannot hide. All the more reason to insist on hypotheses.

Questions from left field

I continue to be amazed when managers, as consultants, ask questions from out of nowhere. Sometimes the questions seem totally irrelevant and then, suddenly, they have illuminated a dark area not even perceived before the question was asked. This happens over and over again. Groups vary, of course, but in the main they continue to ask questions easily and without urging. The sum total of these questions, mundane and exotic, general and incisive, begins to pile up. A pattern, not always obvious, is emerging. The process requires that at some point the process stops and a time-out takes place.

Time-out

Time-out permits everyone, except the Presenter, who must listen but may not participate, to explore her/his ideas as to what is happening within this system. The collective expertise and accumulated experience of everyone is employed to puzzle out the patterns that connect. The roots begin to emerge. Discussion can range over a broad path and there are no limitations or barriers on the sides, in front or back. The discussion is wide open, limited only by the information that is present and one's imagination, to grasp the pattern that connects.

More questions are frequently generated than answers supplied during the first time-out. One moves back into the consultative questioning period, and explores for more data, more information, and, it is hoped, more knowledge and finally, maybe even some wisdom. The question and answer continues until another time-out is called and there is more discussion and exploration. The process continues until some kind of pattern emerges to help explain what has been transpiring. The process is always at the hypothesis level, not at the "truth" level and, one hopes, not at the solution level. One is always trying to get closer and closer to understanding what is going on in the system, not to determine what the truth is and what the truth is not.

Lack of turbulence and conflict

The role of those who participate in an Organizational Role Analysis shifts from Judge to Explorer. When one is asked to examine the role of another person, one is, willy-nilly, put into a judgemental role. Whether we are aware of it or not, and want to or not, there is a clear and present danger of sitting in judgement of someone else.

The use of hypotheses and the emphasis upon the exploratory defuses the judgmental aspect. A question such as, "Did you explore alternative solutions with the boss?" can sound quite judgemental. However, the obligation to present your hypothesis now places the questioner inside the arena. He/she may be wrong and is now open to the same judgement. The turbulence and conflict associated with strong emotional situations is defused. On one occasion we had a boss and his subordinate enact an Organization Role Analysis. The subordinate raised the issue that her boss was too arbitrary and refused to make decisions in a timely manner. The boss attended the session and took up the role as one of the consultants. The Organizational Role Analysis revealed that at the symptom level the subordinate was accurate. The boss was arbitrary. He saw his role to respond to his bosses and change whenever he felt it would satisfy his bosses. The subordinate saw her role to accomplish agreed tasks, which she might arbitrarily overrule if she felt a boss's need was greater.

At the root level it also revealed that she challenged her boss and was in direct competition with him. Her role was to demonstrate that she was a more reliable boss than he was. He was arbitrary as a means of meeting perceived boss's needs and holding off decision-making until the last minute to meet his boss's needs. They had developed a working relation in which they competed. Her role was to control him and his was to control her. They had worked out a perfect non-change strategy to hold the system intact without change. Each held the other responsible for the situation and felt morally self-righteous that they were doing the right thing. She was committed to the agreed task; he was committed to the same task, if and when it was not perceived to be in conflict with the boss. All of this emerged without accusation, conflict, or struggle. No recriminations occurred, but as a result they now knew what they had to do to change the situation and create a positive working relation.

Not all Organization Role Analyses are as dramatic as this was, but each has the potential to move beyond the symptom into the root and area principle.

Ending

The ORA should always end in the same way. At the end of the hour and a half, the Presenter is offered the opportunity to comment on the experience. It is their opportunity to have the last word, to evaluate the experience and to present to the consultants whatever understanding they have reached.

Frequently, real and obvious learning has taken place and the consultants can take satisfaction in their efforts. Frequently, too, there is a limited expression of understanding and sometimes no understanding of what everyone in the room has learned, except it would seem, the Presenter. This is frustrating.

However, within the framework of a *Group Strategy and Action Program*® that lasts 2½ days, it is not uncommon to see the Presenter from an earlier ORA take on the learning and understanding that seemed to have escaped him during the ORA. It is as if he has to let the experience digest and then can allow himself to understand.

Summary

The ORA is an organized process for freeing the individual to understand her role within a system. It is a systemic process, using the system to uncover the system. It requires restraint more than action. It takes restraint on the part of the facilitator not to give answers, not to control the participants, and not to let her anxiety overwhelm her when no obvious insights appear at the beginning. It takes restraint on the part of the newly minted consultants not to rush in with answers, to conform to a process they are unfamiliar with and which appears to constrain them. And it takes restraint on the part of the Presenter to answer difficult questions and to sit by while others make conjectures about her and not respond to or clarify what must appear to be erroneous judgements.

Essentially, the ORA is a system process that functions at the role level, not at the individual level. The process holds the individual hostage, so to speak, in order that the role can appear. Participants frequently think of the process as psychological because it uncovers so much and goes so deep. They label the experience 'psychological' simply because they lack any other language to deal with issues that are experienced as so deeply personal.

Once the role has been uncovered and the relations and rules revealed, it is no longer possible to revert to older roles. The individual has encountered the containing format, the system, and having altered it, can no longer operate in the old system. In other words, the change takes place at the system level, not at the personal or psychological level. It is for this reason that it is called an Organizational Role Analysis and not a personal analysis.

Note

1. The differences between psychology and systems does not infer or suggest that one is truer or more accurate. They are different constructs. One may look at the world from a biological perspective or from a chemical perspective, from a psychological or systemic perspective, each adding knowledge to the other.

CHAPTER TWO

Organizational Role Analysis: the birth and growth of ideas

W. Gordon Lawrence

Since Irving Borwick outlined his ideas on Organizational Role Analysis (ORA) he has influenced my thinking in four identifiable ways. First, he enabled me to make the move from thinking of organizations as being composed of individuals in groups to conceptualizing them as systems, roles, and individuals. This shift opened a new range of possibilities. Second, he furthered the thinking on the concept of the management of self in role, which Eric Miller and I had just started to puzzle out (Lawrence, 1979). Third, he made the concept of the working hypothesis real for me and I have used it ever since in my work. Finally, I am able to see with hindsight how systemic thinking has influenced my thinking in developing new ways of understanding realities, such as Social Dreaming.

I first met Borwick at a Leicester-Tavistock conference on authority and leadership in September, 1973. Subsequently, he invited Dr Pierre Turquet, who had been the director of the conference, to work with him on an ITT programme for senior managers. Turquet died in a car accident in December, 1975. Subsequently, I was appointed joint director of the Tavistock Institute's Group Relations Training Programme. Immediately afterwards Borwick invited me to work with him on his management training programmes with ITT.

Memory is imperfect and subject to the gnawing tooth of time but some incidents remain vividly clear. The initial programmes of Borwick were a mixture of small groups and inter-group events in the Tavistock tradition, based on the original work of Wilfred Bion (Bion, 1961), plus his version of systems thinking. These programmes, while demanding, were also intellectually stimulating and challenging as Borwick led us into a different way of looking at organizations and systems.

The idea of ORA presented

It was around 1976, or the beginning of 1977, that Borwick introduced Bruce Reed and myself to ORA. He drew an isosceles triangle on a flipchart. At the three apexes he wrote: System, Role, and Individual. He proceeded to explain that every individual takes up a role in a system. The way he wanted to work with the management programme members was to take the idea of role and relate it to the systems in which they worked. His argument was that every individual exists and behaves only in roles, which cohere in systems. Starting from the family he explained that the roles change as the individual matures. The role of the infant is different from the adolescent and the adult as the nature of his/her relationships change to other role holders in the family as he or she grows older.

Borwick saw organizations as systems. The idea of systems of organization was familiar to me from the work of the Tavistock and the fact that I belonged to the Social Systems Group within it. However, what was new was the primacy of system, with the result that I was being invited to look at organizations in a new way. The individual, whom I had always seen as salient and pre-eminent, started to look different in the context of role and system. Borwick said that the idea of changing individuals was not our work but, rather, changing systems.

I was astounded at the audacity of the conceptualization, but was resistant. I was being invited to overthrow what I had learned. In particular, both A. K. Rice's paper, 'Individual, group and inter-group processes' (Rice, 1969) and Melanie Klein's *Our Adult World and its Roots in Infancy* (1963) had to be re-examined. I was, at the time, steeped in Rice's thinking, although I felt it to be such a total conceptualization that nothing new could be discovered. Borwick was suggesting a paradigm shift. Certainly, it felt as if I was being presented with a 'catastrophic change' when there is a 'subversion of the order or system of things' generating anxiety (Bion, 1965, p. 8). I was dumbfounded by the brilliancy of the exposition. Reed (1976) published his paper on Organizational Role Analysis about this time, although he doesn't mention Borwick's work.

On that first programme, we worked on ORA. I was hesitant because I was ignorant of how the method worked in experience. I was undergoing a change in my thinking. It was in this context that the notion of working hypothesis became important. A working hypothesis is a sketch of the situation, a guess at what might be happening, a speculation, and recognizes that an individual cannot capture truth because it is too evasive. Bion makes the point that the *noumenon* can never be known for all that we have access to are phenomena (Bion, 1970). The method of the working hypothesis recognizes this. The advantage of the working hypothesis is that another can be substituted which better captures what might be reality.

An interpretation, on the other hand, is delivered with much more sureness and with a sense of truth. That this is spurious and is often projection is not always recognized either by the person giving the interpretation or by the one receiving it. The recipient can reject the interpretation and will be accused of defending against the anxiety of its truth. Hence he accepts it publicly. The argument against interpretation is its sense of not being negotiable. It is also linked to people who give the impression of being omnipotent and omniscient as they deliver the interpretation.

By contrast, a working hypothesis is always negotiable and is much more democratic in that anyone can make a working hypothesis and there is no sense of expertness or hierarchy.

At that first meeting Borwick introduced us to the Mapping Exercise, which was how to begin an ORA. He then outlined the kinds of questions to be asked in exploring role. The individual was regarded as a private matter but it would be possible to disentangle how role performance could be illuminated by the character of the individual. To work directly on the individual was seen as irrelevant and intrusive. At the time, I was suspicious of this move for I felt, wrongly, that this was essential for executing a work role. My thinking was very much determined, at the time, by Tavistock ideas of the individual being connected through his/her inner world to the external environment of reality. Nevertheless I recognized that a step-change in consultancy was being offered. Could I take it?

The first experience of ORA

A few months later a colleague from a business school telephoned. He described a student who was going through difficulties in his family business and was also suffering from bulimia. As we talked the idea of doing an ORA occurred. I suggested that I would work with him on this, but I could do nothing about his bulimia, which I thought his general practitioner would be better able to treat.

Accordingly, it was arranged that David (not his real name) should come to see me. David and I had arranged that he would come once a week for ten weeks. I made the proviso that if he decided to withdraw, we would examine the ending of our relationship. He had to come from Sheffield and I recognized that I was asking a great deal of commitment. I found myself looking forward to my first ORA, even though I knew I was going into the unknown.

> David arrived in London from Sheffield on time. We spent the first part of the session on introducing ourselves to each other. The first task was to complete the Mapping Exercise, which he did.

> The Mapping Exercise, as Borwick had explained it, was based on the assumption that every individual carries a mental map of the systems in which they live and work. This subjective *Mappa Mundi* is based on experience of being in systems. I had explained to David the working hypothesis that we each carried a map that guides and influences our behaviour at any one time in our life careers. Obviously, this map alters in the light of changing circumstance in the environment. I am sure this was the only instruction and I had provided large sheets of paper and coloured pencils for him to draw his map. He was familiar with drawing organizational charts from business school, but I emphasized the idea of mental representation and spontaneity. He spent about twenty minutes on the map.

In that meeting I said I could do nothing directly about his eating problems and what I was to concentrate on was how he took whatever roles he had and how he made them in relation to other key role holders.

We clarified our contract and declared what the primary task of the consultation would be.

Using the map we found he was designated as a manager in the firm, which his father had established. He had an assistant-type role to his father. Father was an inventor and had numerous patents to his name.

The firm specialized in agricultural machinery and while the business was successful enough there was no sense that it could be highly profitable. It was a small to medium-sized company by definition.

This first session was devoted to elaborating the systems he had drawn. Principally there were two interacting systems: the family and the company. There was a third system of the business school. The map was coherent and there was no doubt David had grasped the idea of a mental map.

In that first session we captured the essentials of his situation. Father was the most important in his life. David had one sister, perhaps two. From the time he was born it was clear that he was to inherit the business. David had internalized this destiny of primogeniture. There was a clear overlap between the dynamics of the family and the business system. I suspected that many business decisions were taken round the family dinner table. The family discussed the major decisions on finance and business policy. David still lived with his parents, because he was still a student.

At the end of the first session I felt that the key to the work with David was to disentangle the relationship between his father and himself. In this I was taking an individual, oedipal perspective because I was having difficulty in seeing that the individual was linked to the systems through role. My excuse is that I had just finished my psycho-analysis and was very full of what I thought I had learned. Really, it was about my inability at the time to conceptualize the idea of individual, role, and system; to see them as being on a plane and not hierarchic.

In the subsequent session, a week later, the importance of the family became clearer as the dynamics were identified. David had a sister (I will give her the name of Elspeth), whose husband had the role of sales and marketing in the firm. I imagined the circumstances of the marriage. The family had said that Elspeth's husband had to join the firm. It was his right as he was marrying a family member.

My associations were to the idea of family being of central importance in David's life. By having the husband join the firm any envy and resentment the sister had of the brother would be diminished. Relationships would not be disturbed and the family could maintain co-operative relations as any future potential disruption could be ironed out. I had seen this happen in any number of family enterprises. The marrying of a family member meant automatic acceptance irrespective of ability. Sponsored mobility comes to mind. The idea of the potential spouse having to compete for the role is withheld by everyone in the system. She/he has it of right. Her/his authority to fill the role can never be queried for the purpose of the relationship is to maintain the marriage, irrespective of reality. And so Elspeth's husband joined the firm and was meant to live happily ever after.

David, however, knew that his brother-in-law was "on the take" in that he had been funnelling money from the firm to finance his own business ventures, one of which was a night club. In short, he was embezzling, but because of the family relationship had never been challenged. He was continuing to do so because he knew he was safe from accountability and any prosecution. It would have been unthinkable for the family and business to take legal action for it might have unforeseen consequences for the family and Elspeth's marriage.

We talked of the family dynamics and explored the fact that David had a primordial role in it. His mother and father he loved unreservedly. It did seem to me that he must never upset his father and that this message he had internalized from birth from both his parents, otherwise he would lose his inheritance. Again, I was making the mistake, as I subsequently saw, of conceptualizing and focusing on David as an individual. I essayed an interpretation. (I was still locked into the idea of interpretation, not on working hypotheses, because of my background.) He shot out of the room to go to the lavatory. I determined to be more prudent.

The next major event in the ORA was at the session afterwards. About a third of the way through I made an interpretation about the family dynamics as I understood them, the place of his parents and his place in both the family and the firm. In particular I tried out my ideas on the fact that he had been born to succeed. As a result he had been brought up never to argue, or upset, his father and mother. Therefore, he had missed out on the adolescent rebellion. Perhaps he had difficulty in ingesting the emotional food of his family?

Again, he shot out of the room. I thought I would never see him again and that he had left the consultation, despite my suggesting in the first place that we examine any ending in the event of a breakdown of our relationship.

He came back, throwing himself into the armchair. I asked him, "Do you always piss away your anger?" His reply was to deliver the most sustained attack on the content of the interpretation and on me. This lasted in memory for about ten minutes, for that was what it felt like.

I sat, apparently unmoved. I recall feeling smugly that this was evidence of his transference feelings. I thought, then, in these terms.

At the time, I was preoccupied with transference as I had experienced it in my own psychoanalysis and my work as a consultant at the Tavistock. Transference is the process by which the 'patient displaces on to his analyst feelings, ideas, etc. which derive from previous figures in his life' (Rycroft, 1972, p. 168). Although I knew intellectually that I was not in a psychoanalytic situation, which I was not qualified to conduct, but in an ORA, I still had these vestigial concepts. I subsequently found that the transference could also relate to the system (the organization of the company, the configuration of the family, etc.) of which the person was a member in a role, not only to the consultant or therapist.

An influential idea was Bion's (1961, p. 8) hypothesis that one could see a group from two perspectives. First, there was Oedipus. One could look at the dynamics of the group from the viewpoint of the individual's relationships in pairs (individual/father, individual/sibling, and the like). This could lead into a consideration of the psychopathology of individuals as they interacted in groups. Alongside this, Bion proposed, second, another perspective: Sphinx. Sphinx is a group's capacity to gain knowledge through experience and mobilizes the epistemophilic quality of individuals; the desire to know, being able to grapple with the unknown, or the infinite. This is to focus on the environmental context of the individual; the system that provides being and identity.

This shift to the role perspective made essentially Oedipal, individual thinking redundant. But it was not till later ORAs that I was able to think firmly in these terms. In that first ORA, I was making the transition from an individual perspective to one of role and system.

The session ended. Personally, I was rattled at the intensity of his feelings and my use of the verb 'piss' to mask my anger. I thought that from now on I had to work sedulously on the development of working hypotheses and submerge any thinking on the individual except when it might illumine role performance. This lesson has stayed with me.

The next week David returned. There was an air of confidence about him. He opened by saying, "I have rethought my role and I have decided what I am to do with the firm and what my father's role will be." He proceed to say that (1) he would be managing director from now on, responsible for finance and day-today operations; (2) his father would head a research and development function, which had never existed in the firm, and be David's adviser; (3) the brother-in-law would be invited to leave the company to avoid any scandal, or to mend his ways.

As he outlined his plans I remember thinking on what I had let loose. What would be the consequences of David's actions? I regretted my naïve use of the transference feelings and the paucity of working hypotheses in the discourse. I was filled by the feeling that ORA could have enormous consequences as other people's lives were reorganized. I felt, at the same time, ORA as a potent intervention. Consequently, I decided to test every proposition on role and system David held on the re-organization.

David's father had agreed to everything being proposed. The brother-in-law problem had not been resolved. By David taking over the managing directorship there was some assurance that the company would move from being an extension of the family to being a purposeful enterprise. David, I thought, had dealt fairly with his father. He was an inventor and by making him, in effect, director of research David was giving the authority for father to pursue his real interest, relieving him of the burden of enterprise management. David was also safeguarding the existing patents of his father and ensuring that future patents would be an asset of the company.

We talked of the management of self in role. The idea that each of us has to be aware of and monitor his feelings and emotions to work out what of these he is to bring to bear in his role, we saw as important. About this time David suggested that his mother and father come to see me. Although I was not certain of the purpose of the meeting we agreed that his father might want to talk about what had happened in the company and be prepared to consider what his new role would entail.

As it happened David's mother and father both came to see me. I had some trepidation. Would his father be angry at what was being put in place? Would I be asked to judge David? Would I be seen as an *agent provocateur*? They came on the appointed day. They were a middle-aged couple, both small in height, who, it turned out, were quite delightful. We all agreed that David's plan for the firm would put it on a sound footing since the promise was of financial control. The father was delighted at being able to continue his researches but felt the proposed title of head of R&D was a trifle pretentious. He was a Yorkshire man. We talked of the family and they clearly wanted them to succeed and keep the firm in the family.

About this time David said he was buying a house outside Sheffield where he would begin to live. It was an old cottage and not too expensive. He was enthusiastic and looking forward to being on his own. He had also started to arrive in my office with parcels. They were pots, pans, and other kitchen utensils. At first, I made no comment. At one session I asked him what was happening with his eating problems. He replied that he was learning to cook and described how he planned to have dinner parties at his new house. I did not want to get into his problem, deciding it was beyond my competence. I now thought that if he could take and make a role that had real meaning for him, he would be able privately to think of the reasons for his binge eating. At the same time my private association was that the utensils were 'containers' and that he was beginning to make the move as seeing himself as a psychic container for the business, the family's feelings, and his own future. He was beginning to come into his own.

We continued to work over the next few sessions by my testing his propositions, talking about the ideas that lay behind his decisions, filling out what might be meant by managing oneself in role, exploring what systems might mean and translating what systems might mean in reality. On the penultimate session he suggested that he take me for luncheon after it finished. I agreed.

The last session came. We worked on the feelings that had been engendered in him during the consultation. I talked of mine, particularly the panic I had felt as he made his role change propositions a few sessions ago. We talked of his parents and the positive effect they had had on me.

Having ended the consultancy relationship we went for luncheon. The restaurant he had chosen was nearby and we were able to walk to it. It was a delicious, though for me very substantial, lunch. I noted that he cleared every scrap of food from his plates. We parted.

About a year later I had to go to Sheffield to give a lecture. I telephoned David and arranged to meet while I was there. He collected me by car from my hotel, went for lunch and he told me all that had happened since we had worked together. He was clearly happy and proud as he described how the enterprise was progressing. We then went on to see his house, which he was still renovating though it was nearly completed. We went on a drive to Renishaw to visit the house of the Sitwells, who had fascinated me for most of my adult life. I then took the train to London.

Since the first ORA I have completed endless role consultations with managers, organizational consultants, educationists, and members of Roman Catholic religious orders. I have found role a liberating tool because the individuals can regard role as being outside of themselves and integral to their behaviour in systems. By making working hypotheses on the system the idea of role is situated firmly in the environmental context. It does also lead to further exploration. By never making oedipal type comments the individual is not infantilized, and can preserve their privacy to find and exercise their authority in role. In short, one is focusing on the Sphinx aspects of being; gaining knowledge and understanding to reach beyond the closed system of the individual.

What was learned from the first ORA?

First, that the idea of role being more pertinent in organizational consultancy than that of the individual was beginning to become understandable to me. I was beginning to glimmer that the individual was connected to his/her group, or organization, or system through role. About 1977 I was conducting an enquiry into management development in Britain. In the report I wrote about the distinction between role and job. The department seized on this and wrote a special paper on the importance of role. Role began to become part of the vocabulary of management.

Second, the idea of system, which I then thought to be very abstract and mechanical as it was explained in the text books of the period, had to be imbued with its living qualities. Much later Fritjof Capra was to supply this; for example, underlining the holistic thinking that results from the use of systems (Capra, 1997, 2003).

Third, the idea of a working hypothesis instead of interpretation had to be considered seriously in organizational action research. Interpretation carried the idea of win–lose. The client either accepted or rejected it, or pretended to understand it. The idea of the consultant-as-expert was implicit in the relationship with the client.

A working hypothesis seemed to fit the shared reality better as it was being experienced from different role perspectives. The consultant was giving his conjecture and not dealing in certainty, as implied by interpretation. The working hypothesis takes on the quality of having the possibilities of change intrinsic to it. In other words, the recipient of the working hypothesis can 'play' with it (in the Winnicott sense) and does not see him or herself as having to be compliant with its meaning. That is the essential message of a working hypothesis. As the social world is increasingly construed in postmodern terms, it is congruent with changing realities as perceived from different role viewpoints. In a sense the working hypothesis is the best fit one is capable of making of the complexity of reality, ready to be replaced with another that better approximates what the truth might be.

Further developments of ORA thinking

I took steps to use the working hypothesis instead of the interpretation and introduced this technique into working conferences in the Leicester-Tavistock tradition for it seemed to me to be much more speculative and nearer to how we perceive reality than the seemingly dogmatic interpretation. Furthermore, the use of working hypotheses fosters a culture of enquiry.

I then put up a proposal to the Tavistock Institute of Medical Psychology for a grant to develop a practice in ORA and to pursue the theory further. It was rejected. I cannot emphasize enough that in the mid-1970s the idea of role, except as an adjunct to the individual, was anathema to mainstream Tavistock thinking, which embodied, indeed celebrated, the individual perspective and the group.

At this time I introduced the idea of role analysis into the group relations programme of the Tavistock Institute (Lawrence, 1979), for I found it to be a way whereby people who had had an experience of group relations could explore their learning experience of the conference to link it directly with their work. I called this Systemic Role Analysis because 'Review and Application' groups focused on how the individual was to exercise authority in their organization. By shifting it to role, participants began to glimmer the idea of systems and the mutuality among role-holders. It made explicit a new perspective of how role means that the individual psyche can be monitored and managed in role. This is because role will allow the discrimination of which feelings the individual better hold private and which were better made public.

The idea, central to Bion's thinking, that one could look at a group from two perspectives and have a binocular vision was not present in the thinking of staff. It seems to me now that the Sphinx (knowledge) perspective mobilizes the individual in a questing role for desiring knowledge from experience and through his role performance in the system she/he can work out something of their psychopathology, which is a private matter. In a way, Borwick led me to study more closely Bion's formulation contained in his *Experiences in Groups* (1961, p. 8)

In describing the first ORA, along with my mistakes in thinking, I did not recognise that ORA, in Borwick's scheme, was part of the Group Study and Action Programme (GSAP) that he was developing at the time. There is a real sense in which ORA has become an exaggerated figure, because so many have adopted it, and GSAP has become background, because comparatively few people know about GSAP. ORA, which has been so potent a consulting tool, has been taken out of context since the beginning. It was meant to be part of a process and never a process in its own right. This is not, however, to deny its viability. And not to deny that there will be endless variations on the basic conceptual frame.

Borwick's GSAP, in my experience, is another potent organizational intervention that cuts through much of the thinking that informs, or dis-informs, organizational consultancy. The GSAP is a systemic programme to bring about change in a system (Borwick, 1997). The preparation for the programme is the ORA, which is conducted with individuals. Part of the GSAP is the Role Analysis, which is conducted as an event during the programme. This method involves something like ten people. Specific issues are analysed by role holders, using the others to develop working hypothesis on role performance. Participants are not allowed to ask a question without offering a working hypothesis. The Role Analysis Groups of Borwick's programme become a sustained exploration with never have a hint of persecution. The idea of conducting role analysis in a social setting means that in taking it out of the two person dyad, the resources for analysis and synthesis are multiplied and belong to the participants.

The main thrust of the GSAP is that participants together clarify what they want their system to achieve. Their solutions are taken forward into their business. Over the years I have done many of these GSAPs with Borwick. I am still amazed that they are so effective in the long term and there is substantial evidence that companies can turn round from loss to being profitable. What also amazes me is that the participants understand systemic thinking and apply it within twelve hours of arrival on a three-day programme.

Over the years, Borwick's thinking has affected mine. I am grateful for the opportunity to acknowledge his influence. In particular, I now see the Praxis Event (Lawrence, 1985) as an effort to create a contrapuntal space in group relations conferences whereby participants could develop a task, system, and roles *ab initio*. Similarly, Listening Posts, which I offered to the Organization for Psychoanalytic Understanding of Society (OPUS), when I belonged to it. I borrowed from Professor William Tibble, who was Professor of Education at Leicester University, the idea of Listening Posts, which he had used in his research on adolescents. I had the paradoxical idea that people in the role of citizen could manage themselves into unconscious thinking and so reflect on what was happening in society. Listening Posts worked, but I am sure that they have developed and changed enormously over the succeeding years.

These two experiences were succeeded by steps to the idea of Social Dreaming (Lawrence, 2003), which was the last thing I did at the Tavistock Institute. Briefly, Social Dreaming concentrates on the dream and not, like Freudian analysis, on the dreamer. This is also a contemporary rendition of the idea of Sphinx, gaining knowledge through personal, lived understanding of dreaming, and has nothing to do with Oedipus, i.e., the personal and private. I concentrate on the mental *form* of the dream and leave to one side the mental *content*. Consequently, it is the shared, social realm that is explored, not the private, individual one.

First, there has always been the idea that social dreaming is systemic in that all the dreams are related and interconnecting. The first dream offered in a Social Dreaming Matrix, it can be hypothesized, is a fractal of the whole. The work is to isolate and link the themes that connect the dreams.

Second, the individual is mobilized in the role of the person who simultaneously has the dream and who understands it. This epistemic thrust of Social Dreaming marks it off from other approaches as the individual is relieved from being gagged and bound within the enclosed, self-preoccupations of the dreamer as a system. But I could never have thought of Social Dreaming without the ideas on Systems and all the management training programmes that Borwick pioneered.

In summary, I have outlined the importance of my first ORA with its learning for me and the effects on the client's work life. Also, I have taken the opportunity to acknowledge gratefully the effect of Borwick's systems thinking on my own ideas.

CHAPTER THREE

Organizational Role Analysis at the Grubb Institute of Behavioural Studies: origins and development

Bruce Reed and John Bazalgette

Focusing on working experience: the model and its evolution

Group relations conferences have always been profound experiences for members, and for staff, which clearly affect how participants return to their organizations and begin to behave in new ways in the workplace. The Grubb Institute has always been deeply concerned to understand how the principles on which conferences are designed relate to the everyday experience of workplaces—businesses, schools, churches, hospitals, youth clubs, prisons and probation, and so on. Over the years Organizational Role Analysis (ORA) has become the most powerful way we have developed through which to address the issue directly.

The development began in 1968 when we launched the 'Behaviour in the Working Environment' conference (BWE), an extended six-month, non-residential course designed to give participants time to become familiar with previously unfamiliar ideas and to apply them while in continuing contact with staff and fellow members. The course opened with a full week's group relations conference, including here-and-now events and a Consultation Group. Consultation Groups then met for twelve weeks. After twelve weeks the participants attended the second full conference week that was followed by a further twelve sessions of Consultation Groups.

In this course we made a vitally important discovery

We had been preoccupied with how participants could go about embedding their learning in their places of work. So, in the second phase of Consultation Groups, participants were invited to bring a colleague to the Group to work on a shared practical issue. It became clear from this that, in the context of the Consultation Group, those with no conference experience could get in touch with and work with their own working experience, giving them similar insight into unconscious processes in the workplace as those who had attended the conferences. This realization led to the development in 1972 of what we called Organizational Role Analysis (Mant, 1976; Reed, 1976).

The Grubb Institute's approach to ORA

ORA as The Grubb Institute practises it now provides a professional context for leaders and managers of institutions:

- to examine and articulate their *current working experience*;
- to analyse it in its organizational setting so as to sharpen up the meaning of that experience in terms of purpose, systems and boundaries;
- to grasp opportunities to *find, make and take up their organizational roles* more effectively;
- and thus to *transform* their contribution towards achieving the corporate aims of their institution.

Client ORA is most suitable for those with executive or managerial responsibilities, leading and managing a system of activities, working from a position on the boundary between the system and its context. At the outset of the assignment, they may not be aware in these terms that this is what they are doing, but it is clear from our experience that those who work more through networks than in systems need another approach, which is not ORA.

Time and location. An ORA typically consists of eight two-hour sessions, arranged to take place about two weeks apart, off site for the client. The consultant never meets the client on the client's home ground so that the only evidence available is what the client tells the consultant, uncluttered by the consultant's own separately generated impressions about the organization.

Consultant. The consultant is trained by The Grubb Institute.

Object of study. The focus of work is on the client's description of their relatedness to their working organization drawn from their experience of their day to day working relations and the meaning they attach to them. Attention is paid to decisions and actions that the client takes and how they interpret the behaviour of others towards them, and how these reveal systems held consciously and unconsciously in the client's mind. While the evidence worked with overtly is drawn from the client's descriptions of situations and their feelings about them, a continual area to which the consultant attends is his (or her) own feelings and images engendered by the work. This is comparable to an analyst paying attention to transference and countertransference in an analytic session.

Extravision. Working on a one-to-one basis, even the most experienced consultant is always vulnerable to being captured by the material presented by the client. For this reason consultants build in extravision from a colleague.

Being in role: theoretical framework and its development

Today's practice of ORA draws upon our conceptualization of *role*, a concept for which ORA has provided a development crucible over the last thirty years, where it has been tested continuously against the lived experience of clients and consultants.

A role in our thinking is a mental regulating principle, based on a person's lived experience of the complex interaction of feelings, ideas, and motivations, aroused in working to the aim of a system (which is itself an internal object to the person), integrated consciously and unconsciously and expressed in purposive behaviour.

Limitations of normal uses of the term "role"

Normal uses of the term "role" have limitations:

- They are *prescriptive*. They suggest that a role is largely defined *for* us. This does not do justice to our everyday experience in the roles we have. No one can do a job adequately by adhering slavishly to a job description. Priorities need sorting, activities relating to new circumstances, decisions have to be taken in unforeseen conditions. None of this can be described in advance.
- They tend to be *static*. They do not acknowledge that in taking a role one is always relating to a changing context, both within the organization and in the environment on which it depends for its survival and growth.
- Thinking about "role" in these ways tends to draw a *hard and fast distinction between "role" and "person"*. In fact, great actors acknowledge that to be able to give a convincing portrayal, one must be able to discover something inside oneself that is in tune with the character one is portraying and with the issues opened up by the play.

Taking a role: a dynamic perspective

To take a role implies being able to formulate or discover, however intuitively, a *regulating principle* inside oneself which enables one, as a person, to manage one's behaviour in relation to what needs to be done to further the purpose of the system within which the role is to be taken. So we speak of a *person-in-role*. While a person's inner world has some largely stable elements, much of what is contained there is in constant flux: understandings, insights, feelings, memories, and recognitions continuously interact and affect each other. Similarly, the external world is not rigid, but changes and shifts. Thus, taking a role is *always dynamic*: it is never a fixed response.

This being the case, the possibility always exists for someone working in role to turn adverse conditions into positive ones. We frequently point out that a sailor handling a dinghy in difficult conditions is challenged by the head wind, the height of the waves, the adverse tide and currents if he is to get to his destination. The skill required by the trimming of the sails, the disposition of body weight and the use of the rudder can use these forces to keep the boat moving in the planned general direction. And of course, this is true of everyone working within an organization, which itself has implications.

We can illustrate the principle and those implications with a simple diagram of an everyday occurrence (Figure 1). Imagine two people with managerial responsibilities discussing an issue and coming to what they both think is an agreed course of action.

However, Manager B goes off and in good faith does something entirely different from what Manager A had expected. It is likely that such a thing has happened in most people's experience.

The problem is that each of them has in their minds a different picture of the (apparently same) organization A attributes certain values to what he says and what he hears from B. B does likewise, so they agree on the action, each believing they know what the other intends. But A interprets everything in terms of a "square" organization-in-the-mind, and B interprets the same words and actions in terms of a "triangular" organization-in-the-mind (Figure 2).

The difference between them can be attributed to the way they each experience their work, the values they bring to it and the feelings they have at the time of their meeting. Because they worked with unexplored differences, they had different institutions-in-the-mind. Since some of these were unconscious, they were unable to

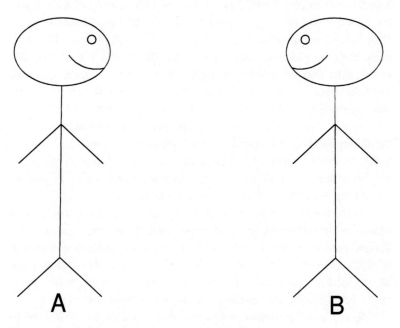

Figure 1. Two people with managerial responsibilities

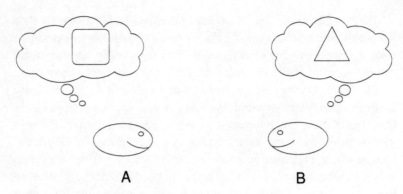

Figure 2. Square and triangular organizations-in-the-mind.

grasp how different they were and how these would affect their subsequent behaviour.

"Organization-in-the-mind" and "institution-in-the-mind"

This model has led the Institute to use definitions about these mental constructs. When people start to examine what they mean by "institution" or "organization", they are trying to identify what they have "in-the-mind" about them. The temptation is always to reify them as existing "out there", but the reality is that they are constructs, and are held only in the mind. We can thus speak of "organization-in-the-mind" and "institution-in-the-mind" (Armstrong, 1997, Carr, 1999; Reed, 1978; Shapiro & Carr, 1991).

Organization-in-the-mind is a construct, focused around emotional experience of tasks, roles, purposes, boundaries, rituals, accountability, competence, failure, or success within the enterprise. Organization-in-the-mind may be more or less conscious or unconscious but whatever it is, it calls for *management*.

Institution-in-the-mind also can be a more or less conscious or unconscious construct, focused around the emotional experience of ideals, values, hopes, beliefs, dreams, symbols, birth, life, death. It is not confined to the internal life of the institution but has resonance within the system from its context, by which it is deeply influenced. Institution-in-the-mind requires *leadership*.

We can say that organization-in-the-mind can be understood as a metaphor of the body, and institution-in-the-mind as a metaphor of the spirit. Together they constitute a whole. A way of illustrating this would be to take the example of the nuclear family. "Nuclear" describes the organization-in-the-mind, and "family" the institution-in-the-mind.

Participating in systems

Everyone who joins an organization or group comes into a particular position. This position may have assigned duties and responsibilities attached to it. There may also be expectations about what is seen as appropriate behaviour (either overtly or covertly). Neither the position nor the expectations define the role, nor do they enable the post-holder to know how to manage his or her behaviour appropriately in the circumstances and situation he or she meets.

A role is fashioned or taken up as a person:

- *identifies the aim* of the system they belong to;
- relates their *own desire* to that aim;
- *takes ownership* of the aim as a member of the system;
- *chooses the action* and personal behaviour which from their position best contributes to *achieving the system's aim*.

Once the person takes the role, they can find themselves in a position to see that the *"taken for granted" aim of the system may need to change* and that by working in role they have *authority* to take action to enable that change to take place.

Since circumstances are always changing, both within the working unit or organization and in the context or environment, a role in this sense is never static.

Role, system and person

Role is an idea in the mind. We cannot see a role but we all behave as persons—all the time. By observing someone we can deduce from how they behave what *system* they have in their mind and what they imagine is needed to contribute to the aim of that system. By "system" we refer to the idea in the mind that, following Bateson (1972), construes human activities as taking place within a boundary that differentiates those activities from their context. A system itself cannot be "seen" though the territory (or space), the membership, the time, and the results of activities may be tangible and concrete.

A *person* is not the same as an "individual", in that an individual can be construed as being bounded by their own skin, while a "person" is a nexus of relationships. This means that a person, without being diminished, may have many roles in the same system when it has several subgroups or subsystems; e.g., in a school a person may be responsible for teaching a subject (the subsystem of a class), have management responsibilities across the school (say, in the pastoral subsystem), and be responsible for the school play (a special cultural subsystem).

A *person* who is appointed to a position in an institution (*system*) and given a job description is assumed to have some of the ingredients for taking a role: the necessary capacities, a grasp of the purpose of the system and an appreciation of conditions, e.g., resources and the state of the environment. They set out to integrate this knowledge and understanding, finding a way of working to achieve the system's purpose. Mentally the person is "constructing" a set of self-disciplined behavioural patterns to achieve the desired goal of this human system of activities.

The ORA process described

Since our initial work on ORA in 1972, we have based our work on the theoretical experiential models of analysis described above. We use a series of working hypotheses to enable clients to have opportunities to work with the realities of their working environment in order to achieve the task that caused them to become our clients.

ORA clients look for practical, not therapeutic, outcomes and accept that they have to find ways of working in their business or institution so that they can make a difference. So ORA sessions are not discussions around theories, but always open up potential for grasping the reality—the truth of the situation—and enabling the client to be in good shape to go and take any necessary action, session by session.

We can now describe the process of an ORA step by step (individually), outlining the key phases and situations that the client experiences over the time of the ORA period.

Finding the role

When we meet as a one-to-one working pair our opening is to invite the client to describe a current incident that points to their difficulties. Working on the realities of the "here and now" of their workplace enables the client to express their feelings about what is happening there, so we at once begin to work on their inner world of ideas, objectives, satisfactions, disappointments, relationships, and a whole plethora of activities and feelings that form the working context of the client.

The client frequently describes a series of linked activities without seeing the whole they represent. They describe networks without being able to identify the boundary holding these activities together in context in a way that implies a clear direction. The consultant may have to tease out the client's working experience in different ways over and over in the following sessions before the client can begin to perceive the "whole" they describe as co-ordinated and having an intrinsic meaning rather than simply being a number of parts that are more or less connected.

This process enables an internal image to surface in the mind of the client where they realize that the organization structure of their institution/business is not "out there" but is a subjective mental *construct* that they can learn to describe and give shape to as details become clearer and the relations between the enterprise and its context becomes sharper.

Drawing on the client's experience, the consultant develops working hypotheses that the client can then use to test realities both during the actual ORA session and back at the workplace. This process is one of the client learning to see their institution as a *system*, an organic series of activities, surrounded by a boundary that differentiates them from the environment. This is a mental image that enables the client to appreciate what the institution is for in reality, discerning what its goals and purpose are in its environment. Part of the significance of this understanding is that the client—especially those with leadership and management responsibilities—begins to become alert to the reality that their executive role is located at the boundary of the system, working to understand and take decisions and actions that influence the engagement of the system with its context.

This process provides a major clue as to the value of the ORA. The effort required by clients to grasp this idea of system is frequently considerable, but it is essential for any executive: those aware of their executive responsibilities soon appreciate that the purpose of the ORA is to enable them to take initiatives on behalf of the system to which they belong.

In other words—they begin to find a position from which to operate legally for the system's benefit as a priority, taking into account all the complexity of factors they encounter in the meantime. The client working on these issues is, in our terms, beginning to work "in role". The consultant's task is to enable the client to describe the system more and more clearly, to define the real results required by that system if it is to survive and grow, and to support the client in locating themselves on the boundary of the system in relation to other executives and operating questions, the deployment of human and other resources, and the sense of being ready to take the risk of going into action.

This first phase of the ORA process is one of *finding* that there is a place for a role in the mental picture of the system that the client is forming, re-forming, and developing, a role that the client begins to believe in and that is proper for him. This disciplined approach acts as a regulating principle for the client in going into unknown territory where feelings challenge the client to take risks with what they are doing—with others as well as themselves.

Making the role

By this time several sessions are likely to have passed. The client gradually orders these working experiences so that they are ready to begin to have a wider understanding of the situation, seen in terms of the system in context. Maybe they have begun to summon up the courage to take action, involving risks, and it is this next phase of the ORA we begin to examine.

This phase is the one of *making* the role, having found that there is one to be made.

It is obvious that in defining the working system the client will become involved with sorting out many overlapping systems—personal, family, professional, financial, among others, all of which have their own impact on the mind-set of the client. These issues arise in sorting out the external pressures as the means of "making the role".

The person in the system. In the course of the sessions so far the client will have been able to check that their experience is that of being a *person* looking for a role, and not just an individual. The person embodies the qualities, aptitudes, character, and competence of the client that is brought to good account in making the role.

Psychological and sociological role. As indicated previously, roles are not seen as such, the only thing others can "see" is behaviour, from which they can deduce its appropriateness according to their own perspectives on the system/institution. The person finding the role may best come across it as an insight—when the system becomes defined with its boundaries and aim. Then the client wants to take action about the aim and can grasp what is necessary for him to discipline himself to achieve it. The two diverse perspectives (person and system) on the client's behaviour-in-role become increasingly important because they influence the client's thinking. The role as internalized by the client, developed and disciplined, adapted and responsive to the internal and external contexts as they interpret them, is the *psychological* role. This expresses the desire of the person, which they bring to their responsibilities, providing them with the emotional energy that they can invest in the work of the system.

But role can also be seen from the point of view of those who experience the behaviour of the client as colleagues, subordinates, or bosses. This is what we call the *sociological* role. Besides the positive experience of feeling supported in their view of what they are doing, clients also experience the possible shock of finding that others express critical and derogatory opinions about the client's behaviour. This can put pressure on him to conform to their sociological perspective, to become anxious, to refuse to take risks or step out of line. The consequence is the client can be compromised in how they work in their roles; their morale can be shaken. This explains why, in the intimate one-to-one with the consultant, the client decides to take an action back at work, but actually does nothing when faced with the awkward realities of the "real" world of work and his colleagues.

Clients usually produce experiences of this kind and the consultant's task is to explore with the client how an adverse sociological role—however powerful—is only one of the external forces that divert the client's focus from his own inner sense of role and his understanding of the purpose of the system. We have given the example of the sailor in his boat, capitalizing on the natural forces available to him, even the seemingly adverse ones.

The use of the concepts of psychological and sociological role have possibilities, that is to say they provide ways for the client to monitor how their intuition or desire is being expressed in the realities of their own behaviour and activities. To follow this through calls for patience and a clear focus on the part of both client and consultant as they come up with working hypotheses for the client to test in practice. Good working hypotheses, tested in the workplace, enhance the client's understanding of themselves and develop how they use their personal qualities. It also furthers their understanding of the real nature and state of the system in which they take a role.

Using working hypotheses

Essential to enabling the client to make the role in their mind is the practice of developing working hypotheses. In ORA, working hypotheses are formulated by the client and consultant together to offer propositions for testing by the client. It enables the client to explore the meaning of the realities that confront them in their system, and to establish in their own minds what is the appropriate role-distance between themselves and others as they prepare to take action. A good working hypothesis reveals the points of leverage in the system that are available to the client and can suggest how to use them.

As we have said earlier, the client's view of the whole system is never fixed; it is dynamic and will be constantly revised. It is also subjective and relative, always influencing the client's behaviour. Sometimes a "story" told in an early session gets repeated but as time has evolved, the meaning changes, revealing underlying patterns that were not apparent in the first telling. Over the eight sessions critical views of others can be explored in depth and may turn out to be based on facts missed at first by the client (and perhaps the consultant). Using working hypotheses about resistances and opposition can finally reveal something that is valid but has been so far unrecognized by the client.

With so many cross-currents of emotion, and often with considerable vested interests at stake, there are bound to be signals that unknown, possibly unconscious, processes are also at work. The consultant can enable the client to address these happenings and to understand some of their meanings by raising the question "Why is this situation happening?" "Why is it necessary for John Doe or Richard Roe to be so uncompromising?" In this way the focus is taken away from John D and Richard R and access becomes available to the hidden forces of the institution, with which to explain their obscurities. So the energies that exist in the system can be released to the client, enabling him to make his role in ways that enable the system to become fit for purpose in its context.

Taking the role

Having evolved a mental image of the system, its aim and boundaries, and formulated thoughts about the system's functioning and about possible causes, the client is equipped to test his thinking by taking action that will in its turn influence the functioning of the system. To behave in role is to *take the role*. Because he is committed to testing a hypothesis that he believes in, the client is both fully committed to what he does but is also open to the possibility that there are factors and forces he has not fully taken into account. So he is ready to learn from what happens.

Over the three months or so of the ORA, the client's view of the nature of themselves as persons and of the system and its aim can be subject to revision and quite new action—which is all part of the ongoing process of understanding and testing the analysis. Each session can contribute to furthering and deepening the client's understanding as he becomes involved in an iterative process of re-finding, re-making and re-taking the role.

Lived examples

We can offer two brief examples of ORA in different settings. In one the client had to revise his view of the aim of the sub-system within the over-arching system with significant implications for his behaviour in role; in the second the two clients came to review how the function of their company was construed, which affected their own working relations and that of the company system itself.

The first case study is of the chaplain in a mental hospital; the other involves two clients, the Managing Director and the Creative Director from the European Region of the same global company, who took their ORAs in parallel.

The hospital Chaplain

FINDING THE ROLE

The client was the head of the Chaplain's Department in a large, internationally known mental hospital. He came because he felt frustrated and marginalized in the hospital, exemplified by the fact that when he presented a Business Plan for his Department (unrequested) the Hospital Board refused even to discuss it. Through the ORA it steadily emerged that he was failing to take serious account of the real boundaries of the Chaplain's Department and the expectations of the hospital management, staff, and patients. Having a therapeutic background himself (besides being an ordained priest) and doing several hours work a week as a therapist, it emerged that he was envious of the perceived status of the therapists and medics "in their white coats": he was seeking to make the Chaplain's Department another kind of therapeutic provision, while denying his theological training and vocation as a priest. Significant evidence to the consultant was that he found himself filled up with images from scripture and theological "insights" into what was happening, while the client was only producing psychodynamic interpretations of what was going on in his work with groups of nurses and patients.

MAKING THE ROLE

The consultant began to offer hypotheses based on his experience of the transference and the splitting that was taking place, sharing these with the client. Having seen these as worth testing, first against other evidence generated from within the consultation and then—once he began to see the probability of the truth of the line of thought—in how he worked in the hospital, the client began to behave differently. This process at first revealed that he felt that his "best therapeutic work" was actually done in the office marked "Chaplain", rather than in the other more clinical settings in which he worked. It became evident that his own *psychological role* was that of a "psychotherapist" and he was seeking to make the Chaplaincy system suitable to realise that desire. Those he met, however, were working with the *sociological role* of "chaplain", were looking for something else from him, and were able to trust him in that role more fully than they could when experiencing him as a therapist, even when he was unaware that that was what they were doing.

By formulating further hypotheses around the interaction regarding the sociological role held from the Board and from groups of nurses and patients, it was revealed that what they were looking for from the Chaplain's Department was a priest and spiritual resource to the hospital, not another seemingly "amateur" therapist. This showed up the tensions between others' expectations of him from his own: they were less instrumental, more numinous and more open to new meanings. They were closer to what he had been trained as and what he was appointed to do.

TAKING THE ROLE

He tested these hypotheses by rethinking his work in the Department with his several colleagues, especially in the hospital Chapel where they devised new services that were more participatory and focused on the real experiences and problems in the life of the hospital. As a result attendance at services increased, and included patients, nursing and medical staff, and hospital managers. Other work was devised that served the spiritual hunger of people in the hospital. Evidence began to accumulate that the revitalized spiritual life in the hospital could contribute to the stabilization and progress of some of the patients who used the Department's services (including one who had made national headlines before he was assigned to the hospital and had proved particularly resistant to treatment to date). There was also evidence of the improvement of morale and effective functioning, especially among nursing staff, who had been adversely affected by a rash of suicides among the outpatients.

The Creative Director and the Managing Director

The Creative Director and the Managing Director had been working together for six months as the Senior Management Team of the European Region of a global agency. The company's business was helping pharmaceutical companies to market their products to the medical world. The two men were referred to The Grubb Institute by the Group Chairman/Chief Executive (GC/CE) because their relationship was deteriorating. The Creative Director was having outbursts of rage, using foul language, and storming out of meetings, apparently enraged by such things as the loss of his parking space at a time of company retrenchment. Meanwhile, the Managing Director was furious at the apparent collusion of his colleague with the behaviour of the members of the Creative Department, who seemed to ignore company practice about working at home, were failing to meet deadlines, and were booking leave without reference to pressures of meeting client commitments.

The impact of the tensions between the two was to suck others into polarized positions in the European office and there was even a danger of splitting the global enterprise. Since the whole company was in a precarious financial state, this could not be allowed to continue. The two ORAs were conducted in parallel by the same consultant after an initial joint meeting with the GC/CE, at which point the aim of the assignment was negotiated. Besides the normal eight fortnightly sessions, two other joint meetings of the three executives with the consultant were planned, one after four sessions of ORA and a further one at the end of the eighth session.

FINDING THE ROLES

In the opening sessions the Creative Director expostulated about the way he felt demeaned and humiliated by his colleague. In his first sessions the Managing Director made it clear that he was only going through the motions of attending the ORA because the GC/CE had said he should; indeed, he had tried to stop taking part but had been advised by the CE to stick with it till the mid-process joint session.

This brought to the surface negatively managed feelings of dependence through which both Executives were using the other to justify their own behaviour, with neither of them being able to find the executive systems that they had been charged to manage, because they had both abdicated their leadership and management to the GC/CE. It was also evident at the beginning of the joint meeting that the GC/CE was colluding with this in a range of ways. It was now that the two ORA clients began to find their different roles in the systems of the whole company. This was assisted by all three executives using drawings and exploring the different meanings of their images.

MAKING THE ROLES

Through testing different working hypotheses, the two arrived at the joint session aware that the dominant psychological role each of them was taking was that of *employee* in relation to the GC/CE, while he was seen as the *employer*. In the joint meeting, the way this psychological role contributed to both of them experiencing a sense of rivalry and lack of co-operation, which they were both causing each other, became starkly evident. Once they began to face this, new ideas about the real company system and its purpose in its contexts began to emerge, and the two of them found themselves in positions to begin to make their roles within it.

This included defining appropriate system boundaries that were managed in ways that brought more discipline into the way their own behaviour was managed. They began to see the reality that the Creative Director had two roles: one leading the Creative Department and one as a corporate member of the Management Team, and there was a natural tension between these two; the Managing Director, meanwhile, became conscious that part of his responsibility was to ensure the integrity of the Regional boundary, rather than to behave sycophantically towards the Chairman. This challenged him to take action about the way the GC/CE had previously behaved, which until then had involved his intervening wherever he wanted across the European office since the Group Headquarters were in the same building. To provide him with an instrument that gave him authority in role, he began to formulate a new statement of the European company's purpose—similar to Ken Rice's definition of primary task (Rice, 1963).

TAKING THE ROLES

In the next phase of the assignment both executives began to take their roles, the one establishing parameters of work that enabled the Creative staff to exercise their imagination and creativity with a sense of freedom, and the other working at developing a concept of the purpose of the European Region within the global company, which included an analysis of why clients used the agency in Europe and also managing the relationship with Group Board staff.

These two reported back to each other and to the GC/CE in the final joint session, which was led and managed by the Managing Director and which was designed around the new definition of the company's task in enabling client pharmaceutical companies' sales and marketing staff creatively to manage their anxieties about marketing their product to the medical profession, whose values were significantly different from those of the drug companies.

The results of the work were of four kinds: the petty arguments between the two European executives disappeared and were replaced by appropriate work tensions between their different functions; the Group Chairman/Chief Executive came to recognize his part in the poverty of the present grasp by the staff of the overall idea of what the Group is as a whole and began work in collaboration with the European executives to remedy this, both in Europe and globally; the European Management Team was used to lead the transformation of the global company; and from a commercial point of view, the European operation has become the most profitable in the whole enterprise, with a reduction in staff turnover and new imagination released amongst the Creative Department.

Systemic theory development

Since places of work are shared places, the internal objects for all those working together are constructed on the basis of experience of the interaction between different organizations-in-the-mind and different institutions-in-the-mind. To explore this experience requires more than a psychodynamic perspective: it requires a *systemic* perspective that draws on psychoanalytic thinking. This also goes beyond systems thinking. In system terms, the emotional experience of the individual relates to the shared experience of everybody in the system, which may be ordered in congruent ways by shared organizations-in-the-mind, generated by effective management of the enterprise. What the person experiences at any moment in time is experienced on behalf of the system and tells him/her things about the state of the system. The emotional experience is important information helping him or her to understand the realities of both images.

To think systemically draws us into the field of the dynamic interaction between systems in their wider context. Here institution-in-the-mind is relevant and questions arise about leadership. It causes us to think about the paradigms of the interactions between institutions, and about the unconscious functions they perform on behalf of society—what Bion (1961, p. 167) called "specialized work groups".

The church is one of Bion's "specialized work groups", and The Grubb Institute has done work over the years on the dynamics that surround churches in a modern society, acting as an object that can—more or less successfully—work at handling society's dependent needs (Reed, Bazalgette, & Hutton, 2002). Drawing on convergence between modern theological research and thinking from the human sciences, we are now exploring the present day experience of the systemic purpose of religious institutions in society today. This includes the potentially inclusive purpose of churches and other religious institutions such as mosques, synagogues, and temples, and schools associated with them, considered at conscious and unconscious levels in societies.

Bion also wrote about the armed forces as handling "fight" and the aristocracy working on "pairing" or hope on society's behalf. This thinking, though perhaps a little dated, gives some clues, though we recognize that in societies that are changing fundamentally, more work is needed to uncover other paradigms of institutions. It is through deepening our understanding of the conscious and unconscious engagements across system boundaries that affect our understanding of "institution-in-the-mind" that we will be able to understand more precisely what it is to take leadership and management roles on institutional boundaries. Psychoanalysis and work on family systems have enabled us to understand more about the dynamics that occur within organizations, but there is much more to be investigated and understood.

While Bion wrote about three "classical" institutions in society; we have many institutions functioning nationally and internationally. We are now in a position to develop more sophisticated paradigms of the functions that different institutions carry out consciously and unconsciously in society today. For example, businesses (of different types), schools, prisons, voluntary bodies, and so on all offer opportunities where we might discover the underlying interactions between systems and which give colour and energy to their functioning. In an earlier paper, Hutton (Hutton, Bazalgette, & Armstrong, 1994) writes about special hospitals and the aviation industry. In a later paper (Hutton, 1997), she offers thoughts about the different functions of different kinds of institutions—police, colleges, Christian voluntary organizations, and public psychological services. Obholzer (1994) also explores this in relation to hospitals and education. Gutmann (1989), in a paper presented to the first Group Relations Symposium at Keble College Oxford, opens up thinking in this direction, focusing on how institutions can both provide societal structures for managing anxiety creatively but can also be used as regressive defences against it. Kirk (2003) makes the point that to work in role is to offer leadership from every position in an organization, however apparently humble.

Since the person takes the role as the "person-in-role" in the system, the interaction between personal desire and institutional purpose in societal contexts is the potentially rich territory that opens up before us if we can identify more clearly these underlying paradigms. Work in ORA along these lines provides a methodology for entering new territory to harvest its potential new insights, which can enhance our understanding of living and working in organizations and in society.

PART II
ORGANIZATIONAL ROLE ANALYSIS: CURRENT VARIATIONS IN METHOD AND APPLICATION

Organizational Role Analysis and consultation: the organization as inner object[1]

Burkard Sievers and Ullrich Beumer

This chapter presents and explains Organizational Role Analysis as a concept of psychoanalytically orientated individual consultancy. Role consultation examines the complex interactive processes between the person and the organization in the context of professional role. A case study is used to illustrate and elucidate the concept. In individual consultancy, the organization is understood as an inner object, awareness of which can help the client to better understand his or her professional role and to differentiate between fantasy, reality, and illusion.

The concept

Organizational role consultation, or role analysis, is a form of consultation for role holders in organizations. It has been developed in the tradition of the Group Relations Conferences sponsored by the Tavistock Institute of Human Relations in London since the late 1950s (cf. e. g., Auer-Hunzinger & Sievers, 1991, Lawrence, this volume; Reed, 1976, Weigand & Sievers, 1985). The focus of Organizational Role Analysis is to gain insight into the way in which the professional role of the client is shaped by the organization and the role holder himself or herself, consciously and unconsciously.

In this sense, ORA can be regarded as a psychoanalytically orientated concept for individual consultancy. As elaborated on a previous occasion (Beumer, 1998), consultancy with a psychoanalytic dimension needs always to maintain a double focus: as well as analysing so-called individual transferences in the context of work, it has to include the interrelatedness of such processes with the unconscious dynamics in the organization as a whole. Use of the term "unconscious" in the context of organizations can be somewhat problematic, as it suggests that psychoanalytical concepts developed through the analysis of individual psychic processes can simply be transferred to organizational phenomena. The dynamics and structures of organizations, however, are so fundamentally different from individual structures of the psyche that substitute terms have been suggested by various authors, including "organizational culture" and "latency" in organizations (Hondrich, 1997). We cannot go into a discussion of this issue in any greater detail here, but the point remains that the focus in psychoanalytically-orientated (individual) consultancy is always the complex interplay and interrelatedness of the personal dynamics of the individual and the psychosocial dynamics in the organization. Organizational Role Analysis, or role consultation, attempts to sustain this double focus (or binocular vision).

From its very beginnings, role analysis has been a consultancy concept designed to help individuals, especially managers, explore the genesis, development, and realization of their role in their organizations. In contrast to those engaged in direct team consultation and consultation to organizations, one-on-one role consultation normally involves no real experience of the organization by the consultant. Instead, the consultancy effort engaged jointly with the client is solely based on analysis of the client's imagination and fantasies about the organization. In this connection, it has proved useful to draw on the concept of the "organization-in-the-mind", a working model whereby the inner images (which are not simply interpreted as personal images) are analysed. With the help of this model, the client is empowered to understand his or her role in the context of such internalized images. Such intensive work helps the role holder in the course of workshops or in a series of sessior.. examine and understand his or her professional role. Individual consultation can never really be restricted to an exclusively individual focus, and—in keeping with its psychoanalytical nature—always has to incorporate various different levels of significance. Role consultation meets the requirement that

> individual consultation with employees—"managers" and "workers" alike—has to look at the formal task and role structure of the company, and it has to clarify the psychosocial dynamics which shape the relationship between the individual role holder and the organization. [Sievers, 1991, p. 272]

This focus clearly distinguishes role consultation from various coaching concepts. Irrespective of theoretical backgrounds and different coaching models, the term "coaching" implies a method that attempts to resolve conflicts in organizations by removing or treating personal deficiencies or character deficits, i.e., by effecting personality changes. Here, internal company or organizational conflicts are seen as personality conflicts and thereby pathologized. Moreover, the learning and developmental concepts upon which coaching is based rely on various forms of training such as instruction, guidance, and imitation (cf. Sievers, 1991). Role analysis, on the other hand, attempts to work with the unknown and the unthought in the organization, and in this way to counter the separation of the individual from the organization. Lawrence has pointed out that many commonly accepted methods in the social sciences tend to legitimize this "myth of separation".

Role consultation, in contrast, pursues a goal of reintegration: "The methodology is concerned to focus on whole systems and their relatedness, and not to be caught in the kind of reductionism that characterises so much of what passes for social science" (Lawrence, 1979, p. 243f.). The decisive qualitative difference is that role consultation is based on the exploration of subjective experience, i.e., on a client's experience of his or her professional role in an organization. This work is based on an understanding of social systems that assumes that an individual's experience reflects more than just the individual, and that the whole and its parts are inextricably related, so that exploration of single phenomena will open the way to interpretation of the whole.

The term "role"

Role analysis focuses on the role a member of an organization has or assumes. The underlying understanding of role is of decisive importance to the entire process. People generally associate the term "role" with the position held within a particular hierarchy of the organization in question, or a description of tasks and responsibilities developed by an organization to define its expectations of the holder of a particular position. More subtle concepts of role attempt to compile an inventory of the open and hidden expectations placed on a person within an organization or group. Models of this kind are, however, too limited to be of much use in an individual consultation context focusing on role analysis. They tend to assume a "prescriptive" character, whereby the role in an organization is for the most part dictated by one-sided definitions provided by the organization and its responsible officers. They also tend to lead to a rather static understanding of role, with little emphasis placed on the dynamic, continuously changing nature of role behaviour in real organizations. Moreover, limited role models of this kind can only offer inadequate, superficial explanations for behaviour within organizations.

In role analysis, we use the term "role" in a more comprehensive, and somewhat metaphorical sense. "Role" comprises, for us, the "place" or "area" that is the "interface" between a person and an organization, or between personal and social systems. The role a person has in an organization is an "area" that is influenced, on the one hand, by the organization and its definitions (other roles, system boundaries, resources, tasks, etc.) and is, on the other hand, filled and shaped by the role holder, i.e., the specific person who assumes and exercises that role. The understanding of role here is not static; role is a part of the psychosocial dynamics that emerge from the "interface" between people and organizations (Auer-Hunzinger & Sievers, 1991, p. 34).

While incorporating aspects of status, tasks and suchlike, this concept goes well beyond them by emphasizing that "real" people and "real" organizations meet in a role.

Pointing to one of the core aspects of this differentiated understanding of role, Triest has coined the terms "formal" and "informal" role (Triest, 1999, p. 210 f.). While the formal role is mainly defined by the organization, irrespective of the person exercising that role, the informal role designates those behaviours by which the person fills the role with personal aspects—both conscious and unconscious needs and aspirations—and at the same time expresses latent role demands or aspects of organizational reality. The informal aspect of role points to the underlying psychosocial dynamic characteristic of this role concept.

The process of taking a role in an organization is, in this sense, seen as an attempt by people to discover how best they can commit themselves to the tasks entailed in their role. Role consultation focuses on the way the primary tasks and targets set by the organization are best combined with the conscious and unconscious aspirations of the person.

This complex field clearly implies tension, conflict and risks, and these are made conscious by role analysis.

Goal: management of oneself in role

The work of role consultation is based on a theoretical concept that assumes that the individual role holder's concern is to "manage" him/herself in his or her role. The concept of "management of oneself in role" was first developed by Gordon Lawrence as a meaningful response to social change. The ability implied in the management of oneself in role is

> that each role-holder is not only concerned with the management of himself in his role but is also having to hold the management of the work group "in the mind". "In the mind", in this context, means that the individual in his role holds a Gestalt of the system as a whole with which he relates from his role, and that he can locate his own work group, as a system with the other systems of the enterprise. [Lawrence, 1979, p. 245]

The concept of management of oneself in role is, in this sense, both an adequate and an unavoidable consequence of the social changes associated with phenomena such as "weak boundaries" and "increasing flexibility" (Voß, 1998). These terms are used generically to allude to a plethora of changes currently taking place in the social organization of work affecting time, place, technology, social organization, meaning, and qualifications. "Weak boundaries can be generally defined as a social process in which social structures that have emerged under certain historical conditions and serve to regulate delimitations are wholly or partially eroded or deliberately disassembled by social changes" (Voß, 1998, p. 474). Both economic and social organizations are transforming social structures into permanently dynamic processes. "Weak boundaries" refers to an increasing lack of specificity in roles, authority, and task. In itself it is a process that has an influence on the psychic experience of members of and the unconscious dynamics in organizations.

As a result of these changes, people in organizations increasingly need to have the ability to develop and define their own action structures; they have to manage themselves in their roles. The management of role is also a management of boundaries, requiring the ability to perceive, define, and handle them flexibly. In this connection, boundary management in relation to roles means "allowing the occurrences of the 'outside' world to impact the 'inner' world, 'relating' them to one's own experience, abilities, feelings etc., and to translate them into 'action', or 'non-action'" (Auer-Hunzinger & Sievers, 1991, p. 35).

The management of oneself in role as a goal of role consultation implies the ability to develop one's own authority in order to interpret prevailing environmental, business, and organizational conditions, and to learn to differentiate between aspects of reality and illusion/fantasy.

The management of oneself in role requires an extremely high level of consciousness with respect to the internal and external forces and demands—the conscious and latent dynamics—on one's role, in order to act and decide as autonomously and as appropriately as possible.

The management of oneself in role is not limited to managers in organizations, even though the complexity of their roles makes it particularly relevant to their situations. The management of oneself in role is a challenge to every role holder in an organization; it is a basic skill that, in the light of the pervasive external changes taking place all around us, will need to be continually developed (Sievers, 1995a).

The perennial question of "for whom" the consultant is performing his or her work is rendered more or less irrelevant using this understanding of role and management of oneself in role.

Role consultation is "understood as an invitation to define the relationship between one's own person and the enterprise in such way that both benefit from it" (Sievers, 1991, p. 273).

Methodology and case example

How does role consultation work in practice? This method was originally developed in connection with the Tavistock Conferences, which have been held regularly in Germany since the 1970s. In this context, the term role consultation was first used to designate a kind of individual consultation that took place within the group. Various methods of role consultation have been developed since then.

The method that we have developed in conferences and workshops over the last number of years entails four steps:

1. The underlying model of "role" as described here is explained to the clients, or participants and visualized as a "graphic interface" of two overlapping circles, one of which symbolizes the "person", and the other the "organization". The overlapping part represents the role.
2. The participants draw their own "roleogrammes" (Auer-Hunzinger & Sievers, 1991, p. 37f.) on large format sheets of paper using crayons. They are invited to use symbols and colours to represent their images and "thoughts". Participants are invited to refrain from writing.
3. Subsequent to a supplementary phase in which further information is gathered and/or questions are clarified, the group and the consultant associate with the pictures in a manner somewhat similar to that used in Balint contexts. Ideas, fantasies, images, comments, and physical reactions from the inner resonance of the viewers are expressed.
4. A shared search and discussion then emerges as to how far person, role, and organization entail interrelatednesses, unclear areas, overlaps, etc. that reveal the fundamental role issue for the participant, or that unveil the unconscious dynamics in the person's relationship to the organization in the context of his or her professional role. Understanding these issues is regarded as a shared process in which the consultant

and the other participants share images and associations, as does the participant who painted the picture.

Role analysis can then proceed over a phase of several individual consultation sessions, using the painting to work through the role issue at hand in specific everyday situations in the organization. In other cases, especially in workshops with clearly defined time limitations, the role consultation is limited to only one or a few sessions.

The following case describes one participant's major learning that occurred in a workshop lasting several days. The area explored was this individual's professional role "at home".

The participant was a woman of around thirty-five who worked as a professional consultant for a consultant company operating world-wide. The woman drew a picture that did not depict the "personal" part as a circle (or semi-circle), but rather as a figure that looked something like the shadow of a larger person. Her role did not appear as an interface either, but rather as a jagged circle that extended into the head of the figure depicting her "personal" part. The organization was shown as a large, in some parts borderless, area. Various symbols in the personal part depicted key aspects, or experiences, of the participant, such as a table laid out with food and wine, but squeezed into one of the painting's extremities. There was also a woman lying down, who was said to be the participant's sick mother, and a heart in a part of the drawing that other participants had earlier referred to as a head. In the role part of the picture, there was a large dollar sign (she worked for an American corporation), in the organization part—rather unexpectedly—a tear falling from an eye.

Interesting fantasies emerged in the subsequent association phase. The role, depicted as a jagged circle, was experienced as an aggressive element that penetrated the person, especially the person's head, and thereby crossed that boundary in a pain-causing manner. The fact that this element was symbolized by a dollar sign—by money—gave rise to an uneasy feeling. The idea of a fist emerged, and the fist was thought either to be punching the person or, interestingly, the very reverse: something to be actively deployed by the person against the organization. Attention was also focused on the shadow figure depicted in the personal part of the drawing. The associations were to a shadow figure, a threatening man and a dark shadow, but did not refer to any specific person. A reference to the American Statue of Liberty was mentioned in connection with the participant's role. The organization, on the other side, was seen as an empty, impersonal entity. In addition to money, the only associations related to the tear, which was impossible to overlook.

What happened in the talk with the participant that followed this association phase? It is important to note that the following ideas might well appear coherent in retrospect, but that in the process of the role consultation itself (which only took an hour), the flow of thoughts came in an entirely creative and spontaneous fashion.

The participant reported that she was not satisfied with her role in the consultancy company. She confirmed that the driving forces of the company were making money and continually expanding their operations. Their view of consultancy was expressed in the association to the Statue of Liberty as the doorway to America, in its constant need to act and evoke change. Borderlessness, or the overstepping of boundaries, proved to be an important point. The participant reported that the organization seemed to be taking her over. She was the only woman working in a team, and the organization used this to demonstrate its diversity to the outside world. She was expected to dress and behave in a feminine way, but the organization did not seem to show any interest in other aspects of her femininity. She felt used and psychically abused in a one-sided way. This corresponded to the feeling that her role, as assigned to her by the organization, did transgress her borders. In the role consultation, it became clear that her colleagues dealt with her femininity in a dominant and consistently abusive way. The corporation worked in the field of consultancy and training, but only with the "hard" aspects of a client organization, i.e., structures, targets, communications, etc. Access to the "softer" aspects of organizational reality, not to mention areas of psychosocial dynamics, were not welcome, and they appeared to be threatening. This description corresponded to the image in the participant's picture of her sick mother, which was interpreted as the incapacitated world of feelings.

But what, more precisely, was the aggressive part in the picture that broke through all boundaries? Further discussion revealed parts of her life story, in particular the history of her relationship with her father, as a story of invisibility. In a process of projective identification, her father saw his daughter as an intellectual "action" woman; in a sense, a man-like woman. She had not experienced respect for, or a trace of interest in, her as a woman. This explained the symbolism of the "shadow" in her picture, which depicted, on the one hand, the threatening father and, on the other hand, the participant's own definition of herself to a shadow, a trace, or a draft. Her neglected emotional, feminine, and pleasurable side (depicted in the image of the table prepared with food and wine) had been pushed to one side. This experience of not-being-seen and of being used for her father's own projections were clearly mirrored in her professional situation. The company she worked for seemed only to offer her the opportunity to reproduce that same experience; i.e., to screen out anything emotional or feminine in the wider sense, and to subsist, at best, as an expanse of projective space for others.

The subsequent work in the workshop focused on the mutual limitations of this constellation. Just as it seemed timely for the participant to free herself from these habitual role demands and restrictions, the organization appeared to be at the same function. Should its consultancy concept be supplemented by a "soft" part in order to achieve more effective results? This would require hard work on the personal role level, as well as on the latent assumptions prevailing in the company. Interestingly, it had already become impossible for her to completely repress these areas in the company, as the trigger event for the present role consultation demonstrated. Recently, she had had a sudden outburst of sadness, vulnerability, and pain (the organization's tear) in the course of talks with senior management and at department conferences. This outburst had been experienced both by herself and her colleagues as alien, inappropriate, and particularly incomprehensible, and was seen as her personal problem, which engendered a certain degree of empathy, but for which there was no real understanding. With the help of the role consultation described here, the context of these emotional outbursts became clear for the first time.

It was also interesting to observe how the dynamics of the fear of invisibility repeated themselves during the role consultation process. One important precept for working with pictures in this way is to ensure that the focus is on the picture and its interpretation, not on the painter. This offers protection and respect for the boundaries of the painter. It also allows the picture to function as a kind of transitional object that helps its originator to achieve greater distance, consciousness, and separation from the original material (Hutton, Bazalgette, & Reed, 1997). In the case at hand, however, the painter was not able to tolerate not being the focus of the exercise and kept getting up and going over to her picture in order to explain points as they arose. After this behaviour was commented on, it became clear that it, too, mirrored her fear of not being seen (in this case by the group or the consultant) and stimulated her to overstepping her boundaries in order to send everyone regular "reminders" of her existence. At the same time, she herself, through this behaviour, regularly transgressed the boundaries set by the consultancy setting.

There is no doubt that her picture could be discussed from other angles, and interpreted in many different ways. For this reason, it is important to remember that work on a picture depicting a role must always be seen as a temporary view, as a light thrown on a specific situation, or on an aspect of role behaviour, and not as a static interpretation, which would be diametrically opposed to the understanding of role set out above.

Let us now look at what this example means in terms of clarification, and what it shows about the essence of organizational role consultation. We will elucidate some of the theoretical concepts that have proven helpful in this context.

Given that the goal of ORA is to examine the interrelatedness of individual and organizational phenomena and dynamics entailed in a particular role, it makes sense to look first at the situation from the perspective of the person in that role. The focus is on the conscious and unconscious assumptions on which the individual construes and forms his or her role. Based on earlier experience, and in accordance with his or her skills, the individual role holder has from the very outset of his or her role assumption an "at least diffuse, preconscious idea of what, how, where, when and for what reasons s/he wants to do, or already does anything" (Weiß, 1991, p. 210). A certain tension develops between the formal role and the processes that evolve from the individual's "investment" of parts of his or her personality in the role. These contributions can conflict with the official role parts, in which case they dominate the actions involved in exercising the formal role. The issues have to do, therefore, with transference phenomena, as became clear in the repetition of painful family experience and conflicts in the case described above. One of the basic hypotheses in role consultation is that a person constructs his or her "'role in the mind' and defines his or her authority with respect to other role holders on the basis of his or her experience with past figures of authority" (Auer-Hunzinger & Sievers, 1991, p. 36).

Taking a role in an organization unavoidably gives rise to an inner occurrence, in which internalized object relationships to important, earlier relevant persons are stimulated. These introjects influence, shape, or collide with the reality of the organization.

The concept of ORA draws on a broad understanding of the phenomenon of transference, which is most clearly described in the intersubjective concept used in psychoanalysis (Stolorow, Brandchaft, & Atwood, 1996). According to this concept, transference is not a pathological phenomenon, but an organizing activity of the person, with which s/he—taking account of all restrictions and opportunities—attempts to re-create the intersubjective field of the (in this case, psychoanalytical) encounter.

> Seen in this light, transference is neither a regression to nor a shift from the past, but rather an expression of the continued influence of organising principles and ideas which have evolved in the patient in a crystallisation process of previous key experiences. [*ibid.*, p. 57]

Psychoanalytically speaking, this means that it can be assumed that interaction processes in organizations are accompanied, or even dominated, by mostly unconscious factors at work in the role holders. The unconscious is understood as another, though not the "real", meaning. As in the case described above, we assume that in contributing to filling a role, the transference of patterns of this kind is not simply a repetition of pathogenic suffering but is also a developmental phenomenon. As such, the process of making these patterns conscious offers the opportunity to handle creatively the challenges posed by the professional role. On the one hand, the role holder senses the temptation to act out a familiar scenario of suffering, but the changed social reality of the organization presents, on the other hand, a challenge to his or her imagination and creativity, offering the opportunity to effect change and to make his or her experience available in actively shaping the organization's reality. For the participant in the case described above, the issue became one of how the suppressed, undeveloped sides of her own personality could be used creatively in her role and in the company. One of the possibilities mentioned in the session was to create an inner alliance with another female colleague from another team, and in this way to lend her own identity more weight. "Transference is the acting out of a person's life drama in the situative circumstances provided by the analytical stage" (Haubl, 1999, p. 32).

Using metaphors from the world of theatre when referring to transference has two major advantages. It avoids pathological associations, and it facilitates a truly intersubjective interpretation of organizational reality, making it easier to perceive one's role as part of a complex reality, of a "wider-reaching work" with changing players, scenes, roles, and stage props. In this metaphorical sense, professional roles present two existential stages or two different dramas. On the one stage, we have an activation of the living matrix of internalized object relationships in the reproduction of the "drama of childhood". On the other, the "drama of work" in the context of the respective organization is enacted with a more or less unconscious role allocation for the individual role holders (Sievers, 1995b). In the case described, the participant's historical background corresponds to the drama taking place in the organization, in which vital parts of organizational reality are repressed, and these two strands blend to a common dramatic play that remains hidden from conscious awareness.

The goal of Organizational Role Analysis, in this case, is to facilitate a clearer differentiation that will make it possible to determine whether the experienced or repressed feelings and the defeats related to them are the result of unresolved personal childhood dramas or part of an adult confrontation with the work at hand, the company, and the requisite role allocations and mechanisms of adaptation.

The organization as an inner landscape

The following section conceptualizes organizational role consultation as a model of psychoanalytically orientated individual consultation. It is worth mentioning again that role consultation is a form of consultancy in which two (or more) people (Long, Newton, & Chapman, Chapter Six, this volume) work inside a special consultancy setting on issues of emotional experience in the client's professional life. The setting dictates that real action, or the experience in the reality of events as they take place in the organization, is not the primary focus of consultancy (as it is, for example, in team consultancy or supervision, in which the team is present on the stage of the organization's reality). More important is the client's relationship to psychic processes taking place in the field of the organization, in particular his or her inner image of the organization. Various terms have been used to describe this inner construction, such as "organization-in-the-mind" (Hutton, Bazalgette, & Reed, 1997), "institution-in-the-mind" (Armstrong, 1997), and "institution-in-experience" (Long, 1999, p. 58). We believe that these concepts provide a useful psychoanalytically orientated frame for the description of the inner landscape of organizations. "Organization-in-the-mind" is that which a person develops as an inner experience and perception of an organization. It is a kind of inner–psychic model of the organization's reality. This inner object shapes and fills the psychic space and influences concrete action.

In this sense, the organization is more an accumulation of experiences that structure the psychic space of the person in question than something outside the person. When we assume a role in an organization, we introject parts of the events around us and create, in accordance with the concept of Melanie Klein, inner objects and part-objects. These objects form an inner matrix that is partially conscious and that must, due to its threatening character, remain partially unconscious. Role consultation is about this inner model, the "organization-in-the-mind". It is important not to see this inner model as something purely personal or to interpret it as a kind of distortion. The role holder's experience as a person provides the "containment" for a vital facet of the organization's inner–psychic space and of interactions taking place therein. The person becomes a kind of container of experience in the life of the organization. In this sense, everything of significance in the role consultation can be interpreted as a reflection of the life of the organization and can be related to it, just as all phenomena occurring in individual analysis can be seen as related to the transference taking place in the analysis.

The inner object of the "organization-in-the-mind" is, therefore, created and discovered in a double sense. In many cases, especially in the experiences discussed in the course of organizational role consultation, the issue is an "unthought known" (as Lawrence [2000, p. 11f.], in further development of Bollas [1987, 1992] has phrased it), i.e., it is about parts of the psychic reality of the organization that are known at a certain level, but cannot be thought or put into words. The aspects of the role, or of the organization, that role consultation brings to conscious awareness are thus not merely individual components, but rather emotional processes that belong to the organization as a whole, though they may have been delegated to a particular role holder for the purpose of containment and processing. The concept of the "organization-in-the-mind" is, however, in our view, only complete when it includes the personal share—in a psychoanalytical sense—of the role holder.

The ideas presented up to now can be mistakenly understood to describe the role holder as an "empty container", as if the reasons for him or her being confronted with specific aspects of the organization's reality were not that important. Describing organizational phenomena as "transference triggers" is helpful, but what must also be included is the drama taking place within an organization as the reactivating moment for childhood dramas. For this reason, we propose supplementing the concept of the "organization-in-the-mind" with the model of an already existing inner "controlling organizational object", by which we mean an inner object that already exists as a matrix for the perception of interactions in the organizational context, and in this way adds contour to the inner perception of the organizational landscape.

König (1986) has refined the concept of the controlling object in relation to understanding fear disorders. He describes a controlling object as an inner object representation whose task is to help the person act purposefully in the resolution of factual and social aspects of external reality. The controlling object comes about through real or fantasized interactions with the early environment, particularly the mother, which are translated into inner regulations and characteristics. These ideas build on Stierlin's (1971) concept of the "gyroscopic function" of inner objects. At the same time the inner object functions as a container for expectations coming from outside and shapes them accordingly. These objects are continuously changed and newly structured in response to external experiences, such as those from the reality of the organization. The question obviously arises as to what precisely do we internally fall back on in our work in organizations and which inner mechanisms are activated when, as in the case example presented above, processes take place that link an inner psychic reality with the "external" reality of the organization. Defining the controlling object as an internalized object that has emerged from interaction with individuals such as the mother, father, etc., might very well fall short as an explanatory model. Ohlmeier has pointed out that the psychic apparatus *per se* has to be understood as an entity with "group characteristics".

> We are obviously dealing with possibilities available to the human psychic life to function in a group, be related to a group, indeed, to be part of a group, and not to exist independently of others as severed, single beings. [Ohlmeier, 1976, p. 1135]

Put in the context of "functioning" in organizations, we can assume that participation in primary family, group, and, particularly, organization constellations leads to the development of key intrapsychic structures that can be described as an inner controlling organization object. This "internalized organization matrix" has a decisive influence on our perception of organizations and the transference conflicts, defences, etc. we experience in our relationships to them. This matrix, together with that which the individual person consciously and unconsciously takes on as part of the organizational reality, forms a complex inner landscape of organizational perception, the "organization-in-the-mind" as we understand the term. We are aware of the tentative quality of the proposed model; closer investigation of the phenomenon could, however, be promising in the search for more understanding of the latent processes taking place in organizations.

Role analysis as individual consultation

In this final section, we will briefly summarize the idea behind and the goal of, Organizational Role Analysis.

The real work consists of uncovering the inner images—the inner objects—of the organization, which have been put together in an "organization-in-the-mind" or, more precisely, a "role-in-the-mind". The aim is to investigate these, and to relate them to the "external" reality of the organization. This is accomplished by a process of hypothesis building, free association, and discussion.

When does this form of individual consultancy make sense and help?

We assume that Organizational Role Analysis is particularly relevant wherever inner or outside developments raise the general level of pressure on the individual role holder. Integration and role identity are at risk when this is the case. Experience shows that the pressure level especially rises when:

- someone takes on a new professional role inside the organization or in a new company;
- changes in the organization (effected in reaction to outside demands or through restructuring processes) call into question patterns that have up to then been accepted without question;
- crises, conflicts, and blockages result from personal life experiences such as a death in the family or the birth of a child.

Role analysis can also be particularly useful in the course of organizational consultations or organizational development processes involving decision-makers, since managers and people in positions of responsibility need to have a particularly high awareness of their own inner ideas of their organization and of possible blind spots.

Organizational Role Analysis is, for us, a concept that takes a more holistic view of the overall "landscape" or drama of work and is less concerned with drawing conclusions about underlying fantasies from individual scenes. This not only makes Organizational Role Analysis an important, psychoanalytically orientated concept for individual consultation—it should, in our view be a part of any consultation process that refers to events taking place beyond the individuality of a client.

Note

1. Translated from German by Michael Power.

CHAPTER FIVE

Organizational Role Analysis: using Bion's binocular vision

Hanni Biran

I n his book *Experiences in Groups*, Bion (1961, p. 8) writes:

> The psychoanalytic approach through the individual and the psychoanalytic approach through the group are dealing with different facets of the same phenomena. The two methods provide the practitioner with a rudimentary *binocular vision*. The observations tend to fall into two categories . . . when examined by one method, centre on the Oedipal situation . . . and when examined by the other, centre on the sphinx. [my italics]

My purpose in this chapter is to elaborate on the concept of the binocular vision, and to build upon it some applications for Organizational Role Analysis (ORA). I follow Gordon Lawrence in emphasizing the importance of the Sphinx for the analysis of organizations in post-modern times (Lawrence, 1999).

Lawrence (2003) deals with the struggle between the egocentric (narcissistic) impulses and the socio-centric impulses (the socialism), which is a dilemma every individual faces. Lawrence applies these concepts to the understanding of the level of thinking in the domain of social systems.

With Bion's and Lawrence's concepts in mind, I try to integrate the important aspects of the binocular vision in Table 1.

Looking at this table we can feel the constant movement—sometimes paradoxical, sometimes impossible—between two opposing poles. These are poles that simultaneously wish to fight each other and unite with each other.

Bion wished to emphasize that as psychoanalysts or as consultants we are not able to view fully and simultaneously both sides of the table. When the consultant is nearing the individual he is distancing himself from the organization; when focusing on the organization, the individual is being marginalized. This is a constant movement. When the individual is the focus of the exploration, we work with the metaphor of Oedipus; when the organization, society, or the group is the focus of the exploration, we work with the metaphor of the Sphinx.

In the exploration of Oedipus we deal with the life story of the individual. It is a biography with a beginning, a middle, and an end. It is a world, which is finite. In such an exploration the sexual instincts will be the focus, as well as the Oedipal conflict, incest, constructing individuality, constructing identity, and object relations. The main links will be L (love) and H (hate) (Bion, 1962).

When the Sphinx is the focus of the exploration, we reach the enigma that stems from the social unconscious. The roots of the enigma are in the trans-individual world, a world of mystery and fate, of big forces that are outside the control of the individual. The Sphinx is the metaphor for a world of upheavals and transformations. The Sphinx disturbs the peace, and as such it is a metaphor for a society in trouble. The Sphinx is associated with collective punishment, plague, war, natural disasters, accidents, and terror.

Table 1. The binocular vision.

Ego-centric	Socio-centric
Narcissism	Social-ism
Oedipus	Sphinx
Past	Future
Finite	Infinite
Establishment	Mystic
Ps (paranoid–schizo) ↔	D (depressive)

The dominant link here is K (knowledge). K-link represents the endless search for meaning and decipherment (Bion, 1962).

When an individual embarks on a search for truth, he (or she) abandons the self's narcissistic and convenient interests. He embarks on a difficult route of meeting with painful truths. The K symbolizes the ability to sustain ignorance and pain. Here we enter the world of infinity, since the search for knowledge is infinite. The meaning of K-link is learning through experience. It is emotional learning that depends on experiences and intuition. It also contains the mystical, innovative, and disturbing aspect, the one that disturbs the universe. This is the kind of learning that, according to Bion (1970), transforms the existing and shakes the establishment.

The play *Oedipus Rex* by Sophocles is the story of a tormented man, torn between his individual needs and his urgent social duties. As the one who solves the riddle of the Sphinx he is the representative of a society in trouble. The social space penetrates forcefully the story of his life even before his birth, allowing him no peace. In that sense, Oedipus is a metaphor for the life of any person who is part of a civilization. No human is born into an empty space. Every human is born into meanings that pervade the social sphere and his parents' house even before his birth. All humans are born into a social fate, sometimes into a curse, a war, or a loss. The Bible says: "Parents have eaten sour grapes and children's teeth are blunted" (Jeremiah 31: 29).

Through the "binocular vision" Bion tries to show the tragedy of human fate. According to this theory, every human being is simultaneously one hundred per cent an individual and one hundred per cent a social animal, and is therefore fated to oscillate all his life between the narcissistic and the social-istic poles. A human being cannot live without society, but nor can he live without an individual identity. The tension between the two aspects will never be resolved. It is impossible to satisfy fully the narcissistic and the social needs, and one aspect will always dominate the other. Therefore, due to the essence of his being, every human being is subject to incompleteness, concession, and uncertainty.

The Sphinx is a metaphor to the riddle of life. Sometimes it is dormant, but it wakes up when society experiences blindness, when a hidden deficiency exists in the social structure. Some disasters befall a society due to an unknown fate, but there are also disasters stemming from the unconscious social aspects, and the Sphinx demands to decipher those aspects.

The enigmatic messages stem from the trans-subjective sphere, and are not under the individual's control. In Israel we experience a constant tragedy. The sons of Holocaust survivors are killed in wars. Innocent people are being killed during routine daily bus rides. On the other side, Palestinians are being killed daily. These occurrences are beyond the Oedipal context. They demand that society will examine itself, and will change the emotional position from one of war to one of peace in order to stop the suffering of both peoples. If that does not happen, the Sphinx will continue to ask its riddles and demand sacrifices.

In a previous article (Biran, 2003), I emphasized the difficulty of moving from monocular to binocular vision in the relationship between Israel and Palestine. The monocular vision is based on a cultural narcissism in contrast to the binocular vision, which is based on the ability to accept a different culture. I summarized this idea in Table 2.

This social and political context influences the atmosphere of organizations. When we analyse different roles and the communication among them, we can feel difficulties in accepting the other and a tendency to departmentalization.

It is important to view *Oedipus Rex* while paying attention to the position of the Sphinx and the importance of the K-link. In the Oedipus story the Sphinx appears as a kind of terrifying monster, whose body is combined of human and animal parts. The Sphinx represents enigma, the undeciphered riddle. It asks a riddle: "Who is the one walking on four legs in the morning, on two legs at noon, and on three by evening?" The answer takes us back to the source, to man himself. He is the one who as an infant walks on all fours,

Table 2.

Social narcissism	Ability to love the other
Impressed by the similar	Accepting the different
Projection on the other	Ability to contain weaknesses and urges
Dehumanizing the other	The ability to defend human dignity
Superiority	Reciprocity

on two legs in adulthood, and uses a stick in old age. Paradoxically, the riddle is banally simple, but simultaneously is illusive and difficult to crack. The answer enfolds the meaning of being human. Man undergoes several changes and metamorphoses in order to discover the human aspect within himself. Often we are blind to something basic and simple that is right there in front of our eyes. The Sphinx is unforgiving of this blindness, and it dashes all those who fail to answer its riddle into the abyss. Only Oedipus solves the riddle successfully.

Enigmatic messages have a Sphinx-like quality. They are terrifying and associated with violence and traumatic experiences. They relate to the boundary between life and death, which is often a very thin line. According to the myth, Oedipus suffered a trauma a few days after he was born. His father Laius, who wanted to avoid the curse according to which his son would kill him, gave him to a shepherd with the order of abandoning the baby on Kitarion Mountain. King Laius pierced the baby's ankles with a pin, so no one would pick it up. The baby's legs were swollen, hence his name Oedipus ("swollen legs"). The mature Oedipus solves a riddle based on the motif of legs. He had to be in contact with an early traumatic experience, which had a monstrous aspect, and which left its mark on his body. In order to crack the Sphinx's riddle he had to return to the most painful spot, to the cruelty he sustained as an infant.

When Bion places the Sphinx in the centre of the Oedipal story, he emphasizes the existence of the unconscious. He shows that the unconscious is endless. Every answer to a riddle evokes a new riddle.

The Oedipus myth is a story of development and growth. It is important to point out that the movement from the unconscious to the conscious is insufficient for creating change. *Consciousness is insufficient for creating a change in our lives.*

In order for a change to occur, a development must take place while tackling anxiety, pain and destructiveness. In order to change, renew oneself, create, develop, grow and live a real life, a human being must continue to ask questions, search and dismantle existing structures so he can build new ones.

On the last line of Table 1 I put the sign Ps↔D, which signifies the constant movement between the paranoid-schizo phase (Ps) and the depressive phase (D). Contrary to Klein, Bion (1963) does not think that the depressive phase is superior in development than the paranoid–schizo phase. Bion believes that a development takes place when there is an ability to move between fragmentation (Ps)—which means giving each part its place and meaning without fearing disintegration—and integration (D), which is the depressive position that views the whole and accepts that which is missing. According to Bion, any integration must be refreshed and resume the dialogue with disintegration in order to reach renewal and fertility. Existing in the depressive phase alone might lead to sterility, compromise, and stagnation. The binocular vision, which oscillates between the two phases and creates vitalization, must be maintained.

Case study

The client. A mental health department of the Ministry of Education, including three branches in different parts of Israel. The department has about sixty employees, who are clinical psychologists and social workers, and it serves a large network of boarding schools for youths throughout the country. The boarding schools educate underprivileged youths from families of low socio-economic status. The majority of the students are from Russian or Ethiopian families of Jews who immigrated to Israel during the 1990s. The schools suffer phenomena such as violence, drug abuse, sexual promiscuity, suicide attempts, and so on.

The reason for the appeal. Dissatisfaction of the headmasters and teachers of the boarding-schools with the functioning of the psychologists and their wish to close down the department, allowing each boarding school to purchase mental health services privately.

The nature of the work with the client. A consecutive three-day, residential workshop. The conducting of Organizational Role Analysis (ORA) groups, using six consultants from the Innovation and Social Change (ICS) Foundation, and an institutional event.

Description of the events

1. *Organizational Role Analysis* group: Each participant was asked to draw his own role, plus the organization in which it was

located, as he had experienced it, while using imagination, images and metaphors, and without using words. Members of the group offered their associations to the drawings. Every participant also related an event from the life of the organization in which he was involved. The participants were asked to relate events that raise a dilemma in their role performance and represent unfinished business.

2. *Institutional event*: In the institutional event the participants built a simulation for studying the relationships between several sub-systems, which were: the department's psychologists and social workers, the schools' headmasters, the students, and the representatives of the ministry responsible for the schools.

In the following I refer to the insights we have gained on the systemic level. These insights refer to the common denominator of the drawings, the events, and the institutional event. Most particularly, we gained insights concerning the participants' joint concept of role.

Insights

1. The psychologists supply a traditional form of psychotherapy. The therapy sessions are exclusively individual, held at the psychologist's office in full discretion and while maintaining no contact between the psychologist and the school's staff, including guides, teachers, and headmasters.

2. The psychologists regard their role as responsible for treating the patient's internal world, and the school's staff as responsible for the daily life of the patient. Such a split is inherent to the role's concept.

3. Violent youths, juvenile delinquents, youths who attempted suicide or are threatening to commit suicide, are all treated clinically, each as an individual case. The psychologists put the emphasis on the patients' past, their family's story and their immigration to Israel. No team was established that would join together psychologists, headmasters, and teachers in order to explore these phenomena on the systemic level and in the context of the school's life here and now.

4. Many metaphors that came up in the ORA are connected with the stigmatization of the psychologist's role as viewed by the school: the psychologist is buried in his office, he lives in a sealed room, he speaks a foreign language, he digs himself into a tunnel, he is afraid to walk about in school's grounds. The metaphors in the drawings included the psychologist's office as a hothouse, a coffin, a sealed box containing treasures, an ambulance running in an empty space, an aquarium, a scarecrow, a ball with a hard shell. On the whole, the metaphors indicated the severe loneliness in which the psychologist finds himself, and the split between himself and the school's environment.

All the above characteristics indicate a traditional role-perception based on the exploration of the unconscious motives of the individual, disconnected from the systemic context. The basic assumption here is based on the Oedipus metaphor, and the binocular vision that creates an interaction between Oedipus and the Sphinx is totally missing. The Oedipal work assumption narrowed the psychologists' vision, causing an ever growing split between them and the schools' staff. The schools' headmasters accumulated anger against the psychologists, who were regarded as not useful. The psychologists were acting in good faith, based on the assumption that places the focus on the individual. This was due to the long years of education absorbed by clinical psychologists, who are trained to be as much as possible discreet, anonymous, hidden, seeing but not seen.

The work done at the workshop

Through the work with the participants' Organizational Role Analysis it became possible to think together about changing the psychologist's primary task, and about changing his role's concept, while revealing the ineffectiveness of maintaining the well known methods of the psychological establishment. The primary task was redefined: instead of the primary task being defined as treating individual troubled youths, it became one of treating *the system* that creates them. It was decided that the psychologist would get out of his office and into the school grounds, would examine the work of the guides and teachers, would hold group talks, would meet with the teams and collaborate with them in identifying problems and difficulties. A suicide attempt by a youth would become a problem of the whole system, not of the psychologist's alone. Attempts by youths to harm themselves, anxiety attacks, collapses, and so on would be examined against the background of the school's life, the systemic relations within it, the timing and the tasks the students must perform. The interaction between the system aspects and the individual aspects would be examined. The aim is to shift to the binocular vision away from the Oedipal metaphor to a different one that has interactions with aspects of the Sphinx.

At the workshop we gained an insight into the fact that the metaphor of the sealed room must be replaced. We looked for metaphors dealing with bridges and contacts. The emerging aim was for the psychologist to create a dialogue between different parts of the system. He should be able to work outside his office and be proactive, not just reactive.

The main conclusion of the workshop was that, in a postmodern world, mental health services operating in complex systems can no longer be provided effectively in their traditional form. The work assumption that is suitable for the private clinic must be changed in a public system that is full of its own pressures and needs.

Once the psychologist becomes a living part of the system's space he will discover new ways of treating the system, and his effectiveness will increase. He will see afresh the needs of the system, and will view the individual's difficulties also as a symptom requiring a systemic exploration. He will assist the headmasters and the schools' staff through an open dialogue with them.

The traditional perception of the psychologist's role was based on the obedient acceptance of the headmasters' requests, without examining the nature and meaning of those requests. This obedience proved sterile. The headmasters were constantly less satisfied with the psychologists' work. The psychologists had left a vacuum in all the leadership aspects of their role within the school system.

The work at the workshop had given the psychologist the legitimacy to become the leader of the therapeutic process, and to become the authority that determines how, when, and in what context the treatment would take place. We reached the conclusion that the psychologist also has managerial functions and not only therapeutic ones. He should teach the headmasters the functions of pain management and anxiety management. Pain and anxiety can be reduced in intensity through correct management. For example, an early diagnosis of problems, and assisting those requiring support and containment through the engagement of friends or guides, before the situation reaches a catastrophic point. The therapeutic and the pedagogical languages must learn to speak with each other. Whenever there is a split, there is no development. The power of the psychologists had been eroded gradually because of a wrong working assumption. As a result of that split, both sides were becoming weaker.

Conclusion

Behind the method of ORA stands the legitimacy to undermine the status quo, to reject established habits, and to reopen questions that have not been asked for a long time. Such an analysis cannot take place without encountering painful and destructive aspects. The analysis reveals a role's aspects that are not under the control of the role-holder. A role is a developing element, and all the changes in it occur on the level of emotional development. A role is a phenomenon that cannot exist in the individual's space; it is always connected with the existence of the other. The interaction between the role and the existence of the other begins in early childhood. Even before birth, when the parents fantasize the child they are going to have, they cast it into a role. In early life the parent is the other in relation to whom the child develops. This "other" changes during life, but its influence on the role remains a strong one. This "other" can also be the organization.

In the ORA, in order to achieve development in the role, we dismantle an existing structure. We return to the (fragmented) Ps phase in order to create a new integration. Meanwhile, through breaking the role into its components, a new constellation is created. The role is being revitalized, and the movement to the (integrated) D phase will occur in a creative way.

The main purpose of the ORA, therefore, is to prevent erosion and sterility, to find new links between the Oedipus metaphor and the Sphinx metaphor, and new links between the mystic (change agent) and the establishment.

When we explore a role we find ourselves in the intermediate space between the narcissistic pole and the social-istic pole. A role contains a combination of these two elements. In order to develop in a role, a person must be satisfied with a partial fulfilment of his narcissistic needs. He must "loan" himself for the benefit of society or an organization. Great leaders who create radical changes are supposed to totally relinquish their personality and be absorbed by the role. The ultimate leaders are those who relinquished their private life in favour of society's needs.

The Jewish Sages tried to explain why Moses was taken out of the story of the Exodus as it is retold in the Hagada, read every year by Jewish families on Passover eve. Moses is not mentioned in the Hagada even once, because the Sages were fearing the deification of human beings. Moses, as the greatest biblical leader, seemed especially threatening in this respect. For that reason, even his burial place remained unknown, inaccessible to those who would seek to worship him. This example illustrates Moses' deeds as a role-holder, who had to operate in the sphere of the Sphinx. Moses was elected to fulfil a role that had changed society, but on the personal level he was deleted, and wasn't even allowed to enter the Promised Land with his people. On the social level he became a symbol, while on the personal level he was displaced.

Most human beings are not the exemplary Moses, but normal persons who must move, and find the balance, between the two poles of the binocular vision. This balance must be disrupted time and again in order to create development.

CHAPTER SIX

Role dialogue: Organizational Role Analysis with pairs from the same organization

Susan Long, John Newton, and Jane Chapman

T his chapter describes a new way of working with the method of Organizational Role Analysis (ORA). Whereas traditionally ORA has involved work between an individual client and a consultant, this chapter documents work between a consultant and two role holders within the same organization. The method was developed as part of a collaborative action research project in correctional services in Australia. It was developed when the researchers were grappling with finding a way for the organization to work with what appeared to be a quite rigid compartmentalization and splitting of roles. Given a proposed reorganization of task in relation to offenders, (*viz.* the introduction of case management) it was imperative that many roles within the service should communicate and work together across traditional boundaries. New ways of taking up the task had to be found through experience. New working relations were implied, but the question arose as to how these might be developed when the culture usually led to "like" speaking with "like" and reinforcing old solutions to old ways of seeing problems.

A major outcome of our work with multiple role holders was what we have now termed "role dialogue". By role dialogue we mean a process whereby organizational members converse: (i) holding their own role and task in mind, (ii) while creating enough reflective space to take in, and work with, information about the role and task of the other(s). Our chapter describes this outcome and give examples of how it developed.

The context of the wider project

The project within which the role analyses took place was a collaborative action research project between researchers from a university and a correctional services organization. The aim of the project was to assist in the development of case management as the organization's primary approach to offender management and development. In contrast to the common method of imposing a blueprint for organizational change from above, the authors were assisting this organization to take an action learning approach whereby change is gradually shaped and tested by those responsible for the actual work.

The general aim of the research was to develop ways of exploring the implementation of case management into correctional services, predominantly through using correctional officers (unit staff) as case managers. Although this staff may be supported by specialist welfare workers, it was the unit staff who were in day to day contact with prisoners and who were perhaps best placed to know the prisoners in their institutional lives. Custodial staff members had taken on many aspects of case management over the past few years, particularly through the use of the Individual Management Plan for offenders and prisoners. However, before this project there had been no systematic way of understanding what case management meant to different staff members, nor any a systematic way of implementing case management throughout the system.

The research task was achieved collaboratively through a series of stages. First, to discover and analyse the existing practice and understanding of case management throughout the correctional service; then, second, working with staff to develop a rigorous operating case management model that was flexible enough to suit various locations and offender categories. The work reported on here was done subsequent to the initial analysis that involved the researchers in interviews with a wide cross-section of staff from a variety of correctional facilities across the state of Victoria. In order to describe the role analysis work, it is worth quoting a section of the report that we gave to the organization management and all those who had been interviewed. What is described here in terms of "isolated roles" was background to the use of role analysis.

An organization has at its centre, *a primary task or set of tasks* to perform. These are the reason for its ongoing existence. For correctional services, this task is "officially" understood as carrying out court orders, which in turn is about incarcerating or otherwise constraining the activities of offenders, whilst encouraging them to address their offending behaviours, with the aim of reducing the risk of re-offending.

However, different role holders or workers in the organization studied engage with the primary task from different perspectives. This simply states that by virtue of his or her role and associated tasks, a Governor, for instance, will engage and work at the primary task with a different idea about that task, than, say, an Industry Supervisor or a Community Corrections Officer. Each role will have a slightly different *task idea* (Chapman, 1999) in mind.

It is evident from talking to people in the organization studied that the *task idea* of managing offenders and convicted criminals was changing. Increasingly, staff are asked to think of offenders and prisoners in terms of individual needs and circumstances, rather than simply as recipients of a unitary institutionalized procedure (such as imprisonment or supervision). This is so, even though the task is "officially" framed in terms of managing orders and sentences, rather than in terms of engaging with people. This is so, even though for many role holders the experience *is* of engaging people; of engaging offenders (often known as crims), whether this is welcomed or distasteful; filled with anxieties and uncertainties or chances for job satisfaction.

The changing task idea seems basically to be *officially framed* as managing a process whereby an offender can take up greater responsibility for dealing with his or her offending *behaviours*. More often, it is *experienced* by field staff as helping offenders to learn new ways of dealing with their lives; particularly within the institution of prison or the institution of criminal justice more broadly. The official framing is often different to the lived experience. The changed (case management) task comes on top of the continuing task of maintaining security and is experienced very differently in different locations, each with different populations of offenders. The task is operationally different in prisons and in community corrections

Interviews with staff indicate that they see the *primary task idea* of the organization as changing. Role holders have different responses to this. What's more, we believe the data indicates that different people are exposed to, and see, different aspects of the changes that stem from the change in task idea. This is not simply because some choose to see one thing whilst others choose to see another. Of course, attitudes come into play, and the interviews indicate that many people believe that some changes are not implemented solely because of poor attitudes. However, we are arguing that different roles *engage with the task* differently and hence are exposed to only a part of the whole.

For instance, security chiefs, or those roles more oriented to security tasks, tend to see case management in terms of security. Industry people, who have through their roles a lot of day to day contact with prisoners, understand that aspect of case management that focuses on the prisoner's needs, say about getting in contact with family, or fears about bullying within the culture. They have a different understanding of the importance of programs and feel the tensions coming from head office about meeting their production targets. They tend to value the industry program as most useful in developing a work ethic and providing a correspondence with life outside of prison.

Many of the people interviewed were able to see the perspective of roles other than their own. Sometimes this was because they had been in those other roles at one time, sometimes because they were clearly willing to think about the connections between their own work and the work of others. It seemed clear to us, however, that the system was poorly organized in terms of facilitating work across roles. Yet this is what is required for a more integrated case management process.

There is a lack of organizational infrastructure to support an understanding by all role holders of (i) their own role and (ii) how this fits with others to (iii) engage the new task idea as a whole. Consequently roles tend to be isolated in the work, with few or no "role bridges" in the structure to link one role with another. At times this role isolation *is* bridged informally or personally, but the need for linking is not taken up in the actual structuring of work.

The change in organizational *task idea* that we have described, and that was described to us by the respondents in this research has implications for the task of case management. Through interviewing many people, we had the impression that different roles were seeing different aspects of the overall task. Some had a much broader view than others, some thought that they had the commanding view, whilst others simply felt the effects of their engagement with the task. But it was only in *the bringing together of the perspectives and experiences of different roles* that the fuller implications of the change on case management as a practice could be understood.

It was through this idea of the bringing together of different role perspectives, that the idea of paired role analysis was developed. Before describing how we effected such a process, we will briefly describe what we understand by ORA.

Organizational Role Analysis

ORA was first developed for work with individual managers to aid them in an exploration of their role as it is discovered, developed and lived within the organization (Armstrong, 1995; Quine & Hutton, 1992; Reed, 1976). It is a method that enables the individual role holder to discover his or her role in the context of their institution-in-the-mind (Armstrong, 1991). This is done through one to one intensive work with a consultant who, through a series of meetings, aids the role holder to examine how his or her role has been shaped in the light of their experience of the institution as a whole.

This is no simple cognitive exercise. Not only is the *role idea* explored, but also the way in which the role holder comes to hold significant emotional roles within the organizational system, and the way the emotional experience of a role has become internally organized as part of what we term the "organization-in-experience: (Long, Newton, & Dalgleish, 2000). Real discovery and learning emerges with a willingness to recover emotional, social, and cognitive meanings within the role and its tasks. This requires both client and consultant staying in touch with the immediacy of their experience within the sessions, as well as their joint capacity for reverie and reflection on material brought to the session from the workplace. Collaborative work is central to such an endeavour, as is a psycho-analytical attention to unconscious processes.

The researchers had included ORA as part of the original design of the action research. Our intention was to do an initial organizational diagnosis (around the project focus of case management of offenders) and then to work with people in key roles to further explore the role and to aid role holders in formulating important areas for change. The diagnosis, which involved individual and group interviews and observations across the whole organization, indicated that different roles engaged with the overall task of case management in quite different ways. Whereas this is not surprising, and one might reasonably expect different role holders to have quite different organizational experiences and frames of reference, the degree to which different aspects of the task were compartmentalized seemed quite dysfunctional. For example, those who worked in industries where many prisoners spend up to six hours a day, rarely spoke to those who worked in the area of educational programmes, where prisoners might spend some day time and evening hours. This was not simply at the operations level but within regional management also. The research team and the project steering group believed this needed to be addressed in the project.

Out of this problem, the research team devised a new way of working with the ORA method. Several pairs of roles within the organization were identified as demonstrating opposite sides of an important organizational split. Role holders were then invited to take part in ORA sessions with a consultant—a member of the research team. Taking part, however, meant agreeing to ORA where two role holders worked together on exploration of each role and the meaning that each role had for each of the pair. We were aware that this move, from a conventional dyadic structure for the ORA to a triadic structure of a consultant working simultaneously with two clients, involved a fundamental shift in technique and focus. However, at that point it seemed like an appropriate approach and we resolved to monitor our work for what it revealed. In the interim we kept referring to the technique as Organizational Role Analysis.

What we did

The research team designed the ORA sessions in a session prior to contracting with the corrections personnel who were invited to take part. Because of the initial interviewing task described above, the researchers knew the names and roles of a large number of potential role holders who might take a part in the process. Thus the researchers were aware of:

- the representation in the sample of roles representing the splits that had been encountered in the first phase of the research;
- the logistical difficulties that were likely to be encountered in setting up ORA sessions with researchers and role holders in different locations, in different roles, and with different tasks;
- the place in the organizational hierarchy represented by the nominated sample of possible working pairs.

Our initial report to the organization had identified the issue of role isolation. Although many roles were affected by the change in *task idea* related to case management, there were cultural and structural impediments for collaboration across roles. Following this, it was decided by the collaborative project steering committee that different role pairs might represent particular organizational splits and that the organizational role analyses could be conducted with these in mind. For instance, some splits noted were between: uniformed and non-uniformed staff members; prisons and community corrections staff members; industries and programmes' staff members; security functions and case management functions; suburban and country; head office, and field staff. The researchers worked with others on the steering committee to select potential pairs for the role analyses.

While we assumed that steering committee members from the organization might be best placed to suggest potential participants, it was only in retrospect that we came to recognize that this assumption itself might be flawed because most of those on the steering committee were from head office, itself only one side of a head office–field split. Consequently, because head office staff members did not always know the exact operational nature of many roles within the organization, pairs were selected somewhat blindly. Further, while some of the pairs selected allowed for the outcomes of the role analyses to lead to new practice implementation, other pairs were less able to do this. Some pairs were more constrained in the work they were able to effect because of geographical distance, their placement in different sub-systems that rarely interacted, because they came from quite different hierarchical positions in the organization, and because they had little authority in the areas where their different roles might interact. None the less, six pairs were eventually selected, each of the three researchers working with two pairs.

Potential participants in the ORA project were pre-issued with a brief description of ORA and its place in the objectives of the overall collaborative action research project. The design of the work was for pairs from roles within public corrections to work together with one of the university researchers for four ninety-minute sessions. Roughly, these were as detailed below.

Session one

INTRODUCTION

- Working with the concepts underlying Organizational Role Analysis, especially those of the organization-in-experience and the finding, making and taking of a role;
- Linking these concepts specifically to the role holder's own roles within the organizational context;
- Connecting the task of the role analysis to the wider collaborative task, *viz.*, through exploration of organizational dynamics and structures, to assist in the development of case management as the primary approach to offender management and development within the organization studied.

ROLE DRAWINGS

Both members of the working pair were asked to do two role drawings. The first was to represent oneself in role, as related to other roles within the workplace, however self defined. The second drawing was from the perspective "as if one were the other".

As regards this second drawing, a methodological divergence occurred due to the three researchers' differential interpretation of "as if one were the other". One researcher asked the pairs to draw "as if each were in the other's role", i.e., demonstrating their own perception of the others' role. The other two researchers asked their pairs to do a drawing of their own role the way they believed the other in the pair perceived it, i.e., demonstrating their own perception of how the other saw their role. The divergence was serendipitous because it cast different lights on the institution-in-experience held by individual workers within different roles.

INITIAL PROCESSING

The remainder of the first session was spent in relatively brief processing of the four drawings done by the role holders.

Session two

The second session placed the spotlight on one member of the working pair. Examined were issues of role perceptions, role idea, role relatedness, and task idea. Also explored were the relationships and relatedness of tasks and roles to other tasks and roles within the organization, and also to the primary task of the overall collaborative research project.

The "spotlighted" member was required to hold to his or her organizational role throughout the session, albeit within a spirit of collective inquiry.

The researcher had the single role of inquirer with the task of facilitating the uncovering of role and task ideas held.

The second member of the working pair had two roles. The first was to join the researcher in this exploration. The second was to relate from within their own organizational role to what was emerging.

Session three

The third session placed the spotlight on the second member of the working pair.

Session four

The major focus of the fourth session was on the interaction between roles. That is, the working pair was required to examine what each of their roles had to say to the other and how that might affect the conceptualization and performance of task. Again, this activity required that participants held in mind the task of the overall project. Role connections were explored in relation to case management as it might be practised within the role holder's specific work location and in the organization as a whole.

The role drawings were used as a reference point and provided subjective data throughout the sessions, but became less important as the data they held was brought into the conscious minds of the working trio—researcher and role holders.

Outcomes

The most notable outcome from the paired organizational role analyses was the emergence and experimentation with what we have now termed *role dialogue*. In simple terms, this means the process of role talking to role, rather than person to person. We will elaborate this working definition after presenting details of the outcomes. Role dialogue occurred more or less successfully in the working pairs depending on a series of constraints. (We will refer to the more negative constraints later in a section on problems.) However, workable and creative role dialogues were achieved. This seemed to be related to several factors, which we will now describe.

1. *Holding to role and the "reflective stance"* was central to the process. The role holders necessarily represented something of a range of abilities to take on board the concepts worked with and to understand the nature of their role within the broader systems of the organization and the overall collaborative project. General intelligence, articulateness, or position in the hierarchy, however, seemed to matter less than the individual's capacity to take up a reflective stance *vis à vis* their own and others' roles. This required holding closely to the roles required for the process and working from these.

2. *Role relations rather than personal relationships* were important. In their ongoing work, some role holders worked relatively closely together while others knew each other only from some distance. In either case, personal liking, admiration, and a similar position in the organizational hierarchy appeared to have little to do with the

ability to get into role dialogue. If anything, dialoguing in role transcended personal likes and dislikes, interpersonal experience, or role distance. Hence, a prison governor was able to understand more clearly the role of community corrections officers and their context for work. Both came to see how different expectations about the development of offenders were affected by the role context, including how factors such as training, gender, and age affected the ways in which the role of case manager was experienced and taken up.

Underlying the emergence of role dialogue was—for some working pairs at least—a developing ability to appreciate something more of what taking up a role means. For most, task meant "job" and role meant "place within the structure". Such a way of thinking meant that role functioning was seen simply in terms of personal capacity and personality. Judgements about this might be made at an interpersonal level. Where the role holders were able to change their role-in-experience through relating role idea to task idea, aspects of the role dialogue themselves took on new meaning. Role dialogue meant that task could be engaged *role-to-role*, so that personal capacity and personality issues became relatively unimportant.

This was important; particularly if the people involved worked within the same sub-system of the organization. While the notion of dialogue had previously been experienced as two people talking to each other, participants were able to find ground where role spoke, and could be listened to because issues of personality were temporarily suspended. The unsurprising outcome (at least to the researchers) of this discovery was that the substance of interpersonal dialogue quite often took the form of gossip about co-workers. The substance of role dialogue, however, was the more fruitful and more enjoyable engagement with task.

3. *The need to move from a position of "role narcissism" to "role centredness" through dialogue* emerged as crucial. By "role narcissism" we mean the tendency in some people to regard their own role as the dominant or most important role within the organization. All other roles are then regarded as subservient to this role. This can apply also to role sub-systems. Thus, an "industries manager" within a prison might hold a view, and a concomitant institution-in-experience, which might be expressed as: "if we didn't get prisoners to work, and customers to buy these products,

the whole system would collapse for lack of sufficient funding". A senior prison officer might express his or her role narcissism as: "case management pays lip service to do-gooders, while we make the system work by keeping the crims locked up". A programmes manager might say: "we are the only people who understand that the real purpose of corrections is about offender development and rehabilitation. Everything else is secondary.". Role narcissism, one might say, fills one's entire role space and leaves little room for the role holder's consideration of other roles in the system.

In the paired role analysis, however, the emergence of role dialogue surprisingly was not hindered by initial role narcissism. Almost the reverse was true. *This was because the clearer the role holders were about the importance of their own roles and tasks, the more easily in role were they able to enter negotiations that are the backbone of role dialogue.* The creative move in role dialogue was from a position of total role narcissism, which disregards the power and importance of other roles, to one of "role centredness". Here other roles are recognized as important, but one negotiates from a position of centredness, strength, and confidence in the importance of one's role. The desirable aspect of role narcissism, i.e., the centrality of role and the consequent ability to stay in role despite the pulls that might be exerted by others to move out of role, aids this process. In role centrality it is as if the initial narcissistic position provides the emotional fuel or background to the work, much as Bion (1961) considers that the basic assumption energizes the work group.

What we are suggesting here is that the process of role dialogue moves the players from initial role narcissism to role centredness, and it is this that promotes good negotiation. We also suggest that role dialogue will fail when the less desirable aspects of role narcissism are not transformed; that is, if players remain intransigent about the absolute centrality of their own roles. Take, for instance, a senior area management team. Role narcissism may be reflected in a fiercely locked-in competition for resources, where persons in roles responsible for particular functions consider only the needs of their own area. Alternatively, dialogue across roles to achieve a satisfactory overall budget and to balance the needs of different functions might be the result of managers negotiating from a role centredness, which also recognizes the context of the overall system. This is not just about developing a common way of seeing, or a "shared mental model" (Schein, 1993). It involves a potential space for learning that allows participants to be in touch with the organization-in-experience that is manifest in their role narcissism.

In the joint role analysis such instances arose. One occurred in a role-based exchange of insight between an industry manager and a programmes manager. The industry manager's double task was: (a) to produce quality factory output at a profit for contracted customers; and (b) to keep a diverse population of prisoners "gain-fully" employed for six hours a day. The programmes manager's task was to work toward the provision of conditions for the personal development of prisoners as a means of addressing their offending behaviour. As colleagues, the two managers had a fairly superficial and defensive relationship in which they joked about their competition for prisoners' time. Each felt their role was the most important in engaging the prisoner, and each had argued for prisoner time. In the paired Organizational Role Analysis, where dialogue occurred between roles (rather than between persons), it emerged that industries in the region concerned were not truly productive because about one third of the prisoners involved were, in essence, unemployable. Further, it also emerged that these were the very prisoners with whom the programmes manager needed to work. The outcome of the dialogue was an increase in the capacity of each manager to engage task and transform role competition into role complementarity. Both roles were required for working with appropriate prisoners. A role-based working relation was formed and enhanced through the development of the dialogue.

Another example was the case of a community corrections offi-cer who believed that the holding of the burden of an overwhelm-ing case-load was what held the whole system, Atlas-like, from collapse. In role dialogue she discovered that she could access support from a highly specialized therapeutic sub-system whose favoured position she had both envied and eschewed.

4. *Working in new ways across organizational boundaries-in-experi-ence and in-the-mind* became possible through the effects of role dialogue. Role dialogue allowed participants to think of their task and role contexts in new ways. For instance, an officer whose prime focus was in the area of "security" began to think about how his role might support case management through his own interactions with prisoners, whereas before he had seen security issues as completely

separate from case management. A senior community corrections officer was more able to take up the authority of her role after role dialogue with a prison governor. Through relating his experience in moving into a general manager role, the governor was able to identify boundaries between different levels of roles, which was helpful to the senior corrections officer in distinguishing the authority and accountability of a "senior" position. Moreover, for this pair, beyond identifying the boundaries of their specific roles, each was able to identify more clearly the points in the system where "continuity of care" across prisons and community corrections was largely non-existent. The result of this was that each was subsequently able to work in new ways with the "other" sub- system.

Another role pair discovered a shared emotional connection when considering the capacity to say "no" as a boundary condition of their roles. This affected their self-management in quite separate roles. The prison officer described part of his custodial role as "riding shotgun over the prisoners' baser instincts, like greed and aggression". For instance, there was a need to exert control over bullying tactics during meals because some prisoners would attempt to take food from others. He was concerned that an expanded role of case management, would threaten his authority to say "no" in such situations. Alternatively, the community corrections officer in this pair increasingly found she couldn't say "no" to the demands created by a system that seemed to be dealing as much with the mentally disabled as the criminal. Through their dialogue they explored what became spoken of as "the boundary of 'no'" and its contribution to the idea of good authority and how this was connected to the possibilities for case management in a correctional services system.

Constraints and problems

We found several constraints on the method used and some issues that indicated those situations where the effectiveness of paired role analysis was reduced and the emergence of role dialogue hampered.

First, the role dialogue may be less effective where the roles involved are structurally distant in the organization. Unless the roles and tasks of the role holders are inherently able to "touch" each other on a fairly regular basis, the process might become at worst a rather empty intellectual exercise, and at best, a shared experience for learning with reduced hope of effecting organizational outcomes from that learning. As with any other organizational skill, role dialogue requires practice and the chance to effect real outcomes.

None the less, this "at best" outcome of dialogue between role holders who have little to do with each other on a day to day basis has advantages if the learning from the dialogue is internalized. For example, a senior prison officer when working with a community corrections officer was reminded of his "acting" role as a staff development officer. Listening to the struggles of the other role holder enabled him better to work on this aspect of his own role. Were he able to take this work back to his workplace and use it as a basis for dialogue with others there, one might consider that the paired role analysis had opened up the possibility of full role dialogue through opening up a new space within his own role.

Second, there existed in this exercise a considerable temptation for the researchers to step out of the collaborative researcher role into the role of consultant or teacher. This appeared to emanate from a belief in the organization that as consultants or teachers we might be seen as "expert" in the field and able to give clear directions to operatives. This would fit with the normative culture and save our co-researchers from the anxieties and pain concomitant with action research, where outcomes cannot be predicted. Alternatively, we believe there was also an unconscious belief that as consultants we might be controlled, forced to "report" and hence become disregarded when we did not produce what was immediately deemed to be required. Moreover, the pressure we experienced to become teachers was exacerbated by the genuine feeling among some role holders that they had not yet been appropriately educated for the practical and emotional demands of taking up the role of case manager. It was important to the creative outcomes of the role dialogue that the researcher held firmly to his or her role as researcher. This emphasized the collaborative nature of the exercise, as the researcher was not the only enquirer into the organizational process. It also placed the experiential discovery of the potential of role dialogue and the negotiations within it firmly within the role holders' court.

Third, the paired Organizational Role Analysis suffered the difficulty inherent in many learning endeavours of how the learning of a few members might become available to the organization as a whole. The culture of the organization under study is characterized by an unconscious desire—perhaps indicative of a parallel process—to keep its members "locked up". Thus, organizational splits are entrenched and the climate encourages gossip rather than dialogue, and competition rather than negotiation. Where participants have been able to stay with the full experience of "role relations" rather than personal relations, the effects of the paired role analysis have been more sustainable.

Fourth, the exercise required a safe environment and a collaborative state-of-mind between participants and researcher. This was achieved in the current research by assuring confidentiality and anonymity. Only general findings were to be reported. Also, the researchers attempted to provide conditions for the sessions that were private, undisturbed, and quiet. Often sessions took place away from the workplace at the university. In any case, the time and task boundaries were firmly kept. These conditions are not easily achieved in workplaces, particularly in the corrections environment, where privacy is rarely achieved for a variety of reasons. We recognize that role dialogue may be less easily achieved in the workplace where such conditions are not present, and where managers, often despite themselves, provoke an atmosphere of "getting it right" (not getting it wrong) rather than of collaborative exploration.

Finally, the experience has indicated the importance of carefully selecting pairs for role analysis. Leaving selection to the senior managers within head office may lead to the process being dominated by a narrow perspective. However, had we left the selection to staff in particular locations, the learning that emerged across locations would not have occurred. Should we do this again, we would take into account the factors that we have discussed in this paper. But then, some important learning often occurs in the most unusual places.

Conclusions

Organizational Role Analysis is a powerful method of working with role holders to enable them, through an examination of the internalized institution-in-experience, to more fully recognize and take up issues of accountability and authority in their work roles. Throughout this method role holders are able to examine unconscious system dynamics that lead toward their taking an emotional as well as a task role in the system. Consequent understandings enable role holders to form hypotheses about their own part in system dynamics.

In the project reported here, role analyses were conducted with pairs of participants from the same organization. We had in mind the splits that we had discovered in the organization, so selected pairs to represent opposite sides of these splits. Essentially, these splits reflected an organization that was compartmentalized and roles that worked in isolation, despite the fact that the focus on offenders was common to all roles and areas. We expected role holders to learn more about each other's roles and that they might learn to better manage themselves in role through such an exploration. We also expected that participants might learn more about the organizational splits identified, and might begin a process of improved communication between roles. We found that this worked well in many cases. Most excitingly, we found that in some instances what emerged was what we have come to describe as role dialogue.

Whereas there were many specific outcomes of the paired role analysis sessions, we do not report these in detail. They were: (a) the many insights gained by participants and applied to their ongoing work; (b) the new connections made by role holders to other role holders, and connections to other roles in general; and (c) the data gained through the process that was now available to the broader collaborative research project. For this chapter, we have concentrated on the outcome of role dialogue as an idea. In this conclusion we will summarize the meaning of role dialogue and how we understand it to be achieved.

By role dialogue we mean a process whereby organizational members converse: (i) holding their own role and task in mind; (ii) while creating enough reflective space to take in, and work with, information about the role and task of the other(s). The activity encompasses:

- collaborative negotiation of role boundaries in relation to a common task, which might involve, for example, regularly redefining the parameters of the task, the resources to carry out the task, the respective authorities and accountabilities of role *vis à vis* each other;

• a shift from the exclusive intrasubjective space of role narcissism to the admissive intersubjective space of role centredness;

The conditions under which role dialogue is best sustained include the following.

It requires a "protected environment". In the collaborative project the University researchers provided a role function to protect the workspace. A similar role or function would be required if role dialogue were to be developed in an organization not as part of action research.

It requires the development of a collaborative state of mind where problems and complexities can be shared, and where an exploration of the institution-in-experience of each participant can be carried out without fear or favour. This collaborative state-of-mind is not readily given, neither can it be commanded, legislated for, nor does it appear simply through goodwill. It emerges from engaging with work where the participants learn the conditions under which they can trust each other.

Role dialogue occurs when participants hold strongly to role and adopt a reflective stance. Without this, the dialogue becomes a take-over by one role rather than a true negotiation of boundaries. Such a take-over may be consciously or unconsciously achieved, but it may well occur when a participant is out of role.

Holding strongly to role may involve a degree of *role narcissism*, which, during the emergence of dialogue, becomes the more creative *role centredness.*

Role dialogue may develop best where participants work in close relation to one another and the operational details of the task can be shared. In any case, it will only occur when "role" talks and listens to "role". This may engage interpersonal process, but is not consequent upon it. Role dialogue can successfully operate between people who are antagonistic to one another personally. The key ingredient is the respect for role and the task from which its authority is derived.

CHAPTER SEVEN

Organizational Role Analysis by telephone: the client I met only once

Rose Redding Mersky

Introduction

Like many—if not most—of my consulting colleagues, I am working with clients more and more over the telephone. This is largely due to the advent of executive coaching and the increasingly complicated nature of people's professional and personal lives. These phone sessions supplement face to face work and generally take place when clients are travelling or are otherwise too busy. While work can be accomplished, it is still considered a compromise. In a sense, it is a "holding action" until the consultant and client can meet again.

For three years, in contrast to this norm, I have been conducting an organizational role consultation by phone with a client I have only met once. This meeting took place over a year after we had begun our work. Before then, despite my suggestions that we work face to face, my client would not make herself available to do so. Citing too little time, too much distance, or too much work, she communicated to me strongly that she preferred working by phone.

Since this was an unprecedented professional experience, I sought out ways to better understand this case in particular and the possibilities of doing consultancy over the phone in general. This paper is a study of the specific dynamics, restrictions, and advantages of work by telephone that may also occur when one does a combination of face to face and phone work with a client. My working hypothesis is that working exclusively by phone does change the way we work, how we undertake our interventions, and how we develop an understanding of our clients and our professional selves.

I will briefly summarize the consultation by describing my client and the course of our work. In the next two sections ("Hypotheses about my client"; "Intervention strategies"), I ask: "What does this preference to work by phone tell me about my client and how does that insight guide me in working with her?". I conclude with reflections on the professional challenges and limitations of this work.

Summary of the consultation

My client, Leslie, was referred to me in November 1999 by a colleague who encountered her in a management workshop and felt ill-equipped to help her. She was described as a very intense, ambitious, and rather cold person with serious difficulties relating to her co-workers. Aged forty-two, with a medical degree and a PhD from a prestigious Ivy League university, she was actively and desperately seeking help for her career. Her goal was to become senior vice president of the global corporation she had been working for since 1996.

From our very first phone contact, Leslie expressed an urgency to begin working immediately and had no desire to meet me in person. Since she had been referred to me by a colleague who had already been working with her, and as she was living in Boston (and I in New York), I assumed that we would soon schedule at least a few direct meetings, so I agreed to begin. In the first year, our one-hour work sessions took place approximately once a week; over the following two years, they took place less regularly. After three years we had had eighty-four sessions (forty-four in 2000, thirty in 2001, seven in 2002, three in 2003).

While we referred to this work as executive coaching, I have always conceived of it as organizational role consultation. In my practice, this methodology is an individually structured process that provides a sophisticated assessment of current role dilemmas, a better understanding of the roles of significant others, greater clarity regarding one's exercise of authority and leadership, and systemic awareness. The goal is to develop more creative and effective strategies for managing oneself in role and to experiment in areas of behaviour and performance that are untested, new territory. As Lawrence (1979, p. 243) states, "the starting-point is the individual in his or her roles in relation to the systems in which he or she lives and works".

When we began, Leslie had a very under-developed idea of role and largely saw every interaction as a personal one. She lacked a basic understanding of the role relationship between superior and subordinate and the important function of containment in the management role. She would inevitably personalize all workplace interactions. Frequently referring to her family's advice and influence, her primary focus has been her intense feelings about her work situation, her colleagues and superiors and a desire to get ahead.

Since we began our work, Leslie has changed jobs three times, each time moving up the hierarchy impressively. When we began, she had a sales support position and travelled every week to the Mid-West. She was extremely unhappy with this position and desperate to get out of that job, feeling it was beneath her. No matter how hard she worked, she consistently felt under-appreciated. After receiving a negative rating from her superior, which surprised and upset her, she soon found a new position in the company as medical adviser to two marketing groups and was relocated to New York City's corporate headquarters.

Despite her evident success in this new role, she experienced tremendous anxieties. She expressed continual doubts about herself and had difficulty holding on to successes as well as coping with inevitable disappointments. After eight months in the position, a letter, signed by her peers, and critical of her working style and inability to work as part of a team, was secretly circulated. When she found out, she immediately found a new position as medical director of the organization's top selling product, which she identified as "the highest medical position in the organization".

In addition to her impressive credentials, Leslie is blessed with many abilities. She has excellent organizational skills, particularly in bringing order out of chaos (she often complains that she has to clean up the messes of her predecessors), and is a superb presenter. She is highly verbal and extremely bright.

What is first and foremost to Leslie is to be seen as the best, particularly by those in charge. All her activities and anxieties are associated with how she is perceived by her superiors. She holds herself to extremely high standards of performance and behaviour and always tries to leave a good impression. "I have to behave a certain way in order to succeed . . . I am trying to avoid anything that is negative". Even when she is praised (which is often), that validation is short-lived and temporary. "If I don't get positive feedback all the time, I am exhausted and tired."

On a daily basis, she works very long hours, getting up at three or four in the morning and working late into the evening. She often works weekends. She flies back and forth from Boston (home) to New York (office) almost every weekend. While she frequently complains about the amount of work, she feels she must respond to all demands and is uncomfortable and anxious if she is not continually busy. Leslie's pattern of "killing herself" is connected to her fantasy that she will be well rewarded.

Leslie frequently expresses disappointment with her superiors. She often copes with these hurts by denigrating them and inflating herself. Her view of subordinates is that they are either incompetent, unwilling to take direction, or lazy. She expresses contempt for peers, who are often a major threat to her ("It is so critical to constantly perform and outdo everybody else"). A peer who gets recognition instead of her can consume her energy, i.e., "Because they make you equivalent, my natural instinct is to crush him. I just want to get rid of him." Concerned about always appearing self-controlled, however, Leslie fears that she will be "found out" or punished for the negative and angry feelings she harbours. "I really have to behave. I have to control myself from really blowing up."

Leslie feels that exhibiting extremely nice behaviours will somehow compensate for her contemptuous attitude and will "coat" the negative with the positive. "I have to mould myself into a pretzel and be sweet and nice." In fact, however, she has little faith in the positive. Even when a positive event has just occurred (highly praised presentation, corner office, bonus) she buries the news in our session. She can often find a negative "spin" on even the most positive event, "They said the presentation was inspiring, but I'm concerned about envy." Hers is a black and white world, where she must be constantly vigilant and on her guard. She cannot relax, even if something good occurs. Often a positive event is followed by expressions of extreme concern about the future. She is always looking for another job.

It is not difficult to imagine why others do not like her. She has made it clear that she hates being around "mediocre people", e.g., "It's insulting being around Alan. I don't want to be associated with him publicly . . . I rarely interface with people who are simple." She often criticizes her peers to her superiors and is disappointed when they take no action and surprised when her peers distance themselves. Her explanation is that they are threatened by her intellect. "My competence makes me more scary to other people." And yet she recognizes that she is part of the problem: "My tone can be very frightening to deal with. I can be condescending. If I met someone like myself, I would be intimidated by me."

Leslie feels isolated "not interfacing with people more similar". She often expresses her loneliness: "No one is your friend. I feel alone in this big company." She is extremely sensitive to being excluded, and when that occurs, she copes by denigrating: "Others are simple. Maybe that's why I don't fit in."

My client brings her family of origin into every aspect of her organizational role. She constantly discusses her work situation with family members and seeks their advice. Her various elaborate explanations for the behaviour of others seem often to find their source in family members (particularly her father and husband), who support her by stating that others are envious or out to get her (e.g. "He's trying to make you look bad . . . She's malignant. She will try to use anyone to her own advantage . . . They are egging you on"). Denigration of others appears to be the most highly evolved and acceptable family defence against feelings of need, dependency, and vulnerability.

What does this preference to work by phone tell me about my client?

I believe that in many ways working over the phone provides Leslie with a sense of safety and control. First and foremost, there is the actual physical separation. Leslie is someone who keeps her relationships at a distance in the workplace and the phone serves the same function for this consultation. As psychoanalyst Linda Larkin (2000, p. 3) writes, this medium affords "the distance and sense of control . . . to manage her fears of being in a relationship".

Of course, one of the major drawbacks of working by phone is that the "visual clues of each participant are missing such as gesture, posture, dress, grooming, eye contact etc. Even the fragrance of each participant is missing" (Manosevitz, 2000, p. 6). At the most basic, because I cannot read her facial expressions or body language, working over the phone helps her to feel that she can manage my impressions of her more easily than the effort required to do so in the workplace, where she feels she must constantly "be on" and where "they watch everything you do and what you wear". This has helped me to understand why someone who so craves to be seen is so unwilling to be seen by me.

As previously noted, Leslie is highly critical of others as well as highly anxious about being criticized. Working by phone eliminates the possibility of criticism of her physical appearance and behaviour. It helps her to be more disguised and anonymous, thus giving her a feeling of being less vulnerable.

Our one meeting, at the client's initiative, took place a year after our work began. She was concerned about the way she makes eye contact ("too intense") and how she generally relates to people in person. Despite her stated goal for the meeting, it was difficult for her to maintain eye contact and she was reluctant to address the topic. Not only was she a glamorous "eyeful", she was quite formal and distant. Since then, she has made no further suggestions that we meet and has not responded to mine.

Leslie's control starts at the beginning of each work session, when she makes the phone call. Leslie does any manner of tasks (I often hear ice clinking) and even activities that directly compete (e.g., checking her e-mails) while we are working. This gives her the opportunity to act out her ambivalence to our work and retain the illusion that she is controlling my experience of her.

I believe that working by phone provides her with a certain freedom to use expressive, spontaneous language and to behave in ways she might not in person. As Sulkowicz (2000, p. 1) notes, it creates a "spirit of disinhibition". Thus, I have access to a part of her that might not otherwise find expression in a face to face relationship. Assuming that she feels safer over the phone, I take it that she is offering me material that she otherwise keeps to herself and of which she is perhaps unaware. On balance, however, I would suggest that the dilution of our work resulting from the distance of the phone probably outweighs this potential benefit.

The use of the telephone makes it possible for Leslie to keep me, and the consultation, separate from her workplace and her family. Because I am not "contaminated" by associations with others in those environments, the consultation and I can be maintained as "good" objects. As Civin (2000, p. 196) writes:

> In the presence of abundant experience of persecutory anxiety, an individual might try to use splitting to attempt to preserve loving experience from contamination by hateful experience, to save love from the external environment from contamination by internal foulness or vice versa.

This need for splitting, however, is often accompanied by a "simultaneous desire for wholeness that contradicts the desire for security" (ibid., p. 193). I believe that Leslie carries a similar tension, i.e., the desire for integration and the need to keep things separate for safety. I see this, for example, in the integration that seems to occur following my establishment of various boundaries during the course of our working relationship.

The answering machine has been an integral part of the consultation, as it provides reliable contact with me. Whenever she calls, she knows she will hear my voice—either live or on the machine. As Aronson (1996, p.164) observes:

> On the machine the therapist's voice was always present in a totally predictable way and the illusion of constant availability could be maintained. Speaking aloud to the machine was entirely under the patient's control ... [It] allowed her to speak to me as if I were present and as if I were her omnipotent creation ... Just as with a teddy bear, there was the illusion of the responsive object.

For Leslie, I believe there is a need for constant access. There have been times when she has called me directly after a difficult experience and has wanted to immediately book an appointment for that day. It has been my experience as an organizational consultant that many clients simply cannot commit to a regular schedule of appointments; sometimes there is a need for more flexible availability. Because we work by phone, Leslie and I have that flexibility.

One great asset of working over the phone is the stability and containment it provides. Were we to be holding regular face to face sessions, our busy work and travel schedules would force us to cancel or rearrange many of them. Despite our busy schedules, we are generally able to talk the same time each week. As Zalusky (1998, p. 10) notes: "No matter where she was she could always maintain connectedness to an emotionally present person, even if I were in a distant city . . . [providing] an ever increasing sense of object constancy". For Leslie I believe this constancy is particularly important due to her feelings of visibility and vulnerability in the organizational environment. This is especially necessary when she is in the midst of unpredictable or socially demanding circumstances, such as at off-sites, conferences, or week-long sales meetings.

Intervention strategies

This consultation has challenged me to develop new ways of working. One major difficulty is that I am not on site and cannot observe how Leslie interacts with others, much less conduct interviews to assess how she is perceived by her subordinates, superiors, and peers. Since our work is not sanctioned organizationally (she pays the fee), there is no opportunity to interface with her superiors and set goals in alignment with their priorities. Unable to collect this data and present it to her for her learning, I must rely on what others have written about her. Except through her perceptions, I don't really have a sense of the organizational culture and how my client's behaviour contrasts or fits in with the norm (she is my only client from this organization.). I must rely on the information she shares about her organization, even as she acknowledges her limited understanding ("I don't get it politically").

Having limited access to organizational data is a persistent issue in role consultation, even when a consultant works on site. Often all one gets is the client's perspective, so the challenge is to understand the client's internalized organization, or what Armstrong terms the "organization in the mind" (Armstrong, 1995). My essential hypothesis is that the organization in Leslie's mind is the unexplored and therefore unresolved ordeal of her childhood. She projects her chaotic internal world on to the organization, and whatever is projected out is then reintrojected. I believe Leslie's self criticism is projected on to her superiors, whose criticism she constantly fears, and on to colleagues and subordinates towards whom she expresses contempt. She is unable to assess and understand the behaviour of others except in relationship to this internal world. Under these circumstances, it is understandable that concepts of role, role relationships, and systemic issues would be extremely difficult to integrate.

Working by phone places new demands on the consultant and requires an "active and inquisitive stance" (Zalusky, 1998, p. 7) in order to hear the nuances of thinking and associations. Without the countless physical clues of connection, I am more aware when my attention is straying. I must listen and listen carefully to her, and often reassure her (and myself) of my presence and the continuity of her experience in me by referring to something she has previously said or done. (I often refer to her original goals and strategies, as well as examples of success.)

Unable to rely on visual landmarks, both Leslie and I are more dependent on words. The tone of voice, the length of silences, the comparative amount of talk take on particular significance over the phone. Leslie is a very verbal and articulate person, which is good. For someone so highly verbal, working by phone is a natural vehicle. However, she also uses language to fill up the space and control the interaction, which often leaves no space for thinking, reflection, or spontaneity. For example, she begins each session with a ritualized summary of her current situation, which seems to be the verbal equivalent of the thoughts constantly going on in her head. While this helps her contain whatever anxiety she experiences at our initial contact, I have few possibilities for intervening other than to interrupt her. She cannot see the facial expression associated with my attempts to ask a question or make an observation. When I don't interrupt her and simply listen, I find myself quite depleted by the time she stops. Giving her feedback on this experience has helped her realize how her organizational colleagues may also feel.

This high attention to language provides an expanded window into the material Leslie presents. Her vocabulary is studded with words regarding how she is perceived. Not surprisingly, it is also replete with words and phrases expressing her denigration of others: e.g., "way too simple", "manipulative", "stupid", "abusive", "controlling", "inappropriate". From her language, I have developed a picture of her internal world as one which is under constant siege from a hostile and difficult external environment. On the one hand, she must always be on guard, and on the other, infinitely flexible.

On a practical level, working by phone has some distinct advantages. Because I wear a headset when we work, I am able to write notes of our sessions using her exact words. Thus, I have a verbal "picture" of my client that I would not otherwise have were we working face to face and I had to reconstruct each session afterwards. Because I am already taking notes on the PC during each session, I have been more disciplined and consistent in writing up my notes.

Leslie knows that I am writing while we work; I asked for her permission to do so in advance and told her it was for my own records. For the first six months, I sent her written notes of our sessions. I believe this gave her a sense of containment and also the reassurance that she was being listened to and understood. While she does pick up my language in the course of a session, she mostly needs to put her wishes and resolves into her own words. Leslie seems to find particular comfort in talking and in presenting her view of the situation. When she cannot continue, she often asks: "What can I say?", as if there must be words somewhere to describe her experiences. I often refer to her language in later sessions. Thus, her own vocabulary and language serves as one method of providing continuity and demonstrating progress in this long-term working relationship.

We began the consultation with Leslie's goal of becoming a senior vice president, which remains constant. Over time we have articulated a strategy to get there, which has been continually updated in writing. (My early suggestion that she consider other possible goals was not taken up by her. I think part of the way she contains herself emotionally is to hold on to a steady and dependable—though perhaps unrealistic—goal.) Often she becomes doubtful about her inevitable success and concerned about her present circumstances. In these situations, I refer to the original strategy and note what she has accomplished toward her goals. In the absence of face to face experience with one another, the strategy document takes on the role of a constant reference point. Referring to it helps her to disengage from the immediate situation, which is consuming her, and to re-engage with the bigger picture. This often calms and mobilizes her.

While my client's goal is to be a vice president, I do not work with the same goal in mind. Without direct observation or data from the system, I cannot evaluate her capacity to take such a role or judge her chances of success. Additionally, the system itself has not contracted with me to help her achieve this goal. As I said in the introduction, my goal is to help her develop a capacity to explore issues from the perspective of her organizational role and to understand herself in the larger system. Whenever possible, I offer organizational hypotheses for situations she encounters and cannot understand. Because I have no direct data, I am quite free to experiment with hypotheses from the others' perspective. For example, I might speculate that a critical superior has anxieties about pleasing her or that a peer who has distanced him/herself may feel quite uncertain how to develop a relationship with her. I frequently invite Leslie to develop her own hypotheses.

A client's relationship with a consultant can be compared to her relationships to the primary players in her life. One could say that the issues and transactions in this relationship are enactments of issues in the client's past. When they are noted and worked through, they illuminate the client's internal world and can result in positive change (Mersky, 2001). There is less opportunity for that material to arise when working over the phone, so I pay a great deal of attention to all boundary issues between us, in order to identify possible enactments that can lead us to some insight. For example, there was a period of time when my client would talk beyond the scheduled end of the hour, as if we had unlimited time. I felt abused by her and yet somehow powerless to speak up. Feeling particularly hopeless one evening, I admitted my confusion and helplessness. This led her to reflect on recent experiences with a superior who continually hangs around her office. She has not known what to say to him. We realized that I was having a parallel experience to the one that she was having with her superior. After that episode, she would often anticipate the impending end of a session and would take the initiative to conclude it on time. I began to realize the effectiveness of this intervention, because each time I held a boundary in our relationship or attempted in retrospect to explore a transaction between us, I found her to be more amenable and reflective. Following those interventions, the most progress seems to have been made.

Conclusion: the professional challenges of this work

I believe that face to face work is always preferable to working by phone. On the other hand, I have learned from this consultation that it is still possible to do something useful using this medium exclusively. As Sulkowicz (2000, p. 12) puts it: "It's not optimal, or the gold standard, but it works."

The feedback and supervision I have received has helped me to maintain clarity regarding my goal for this consultation, which is to help Leslie to develop a capacity to explore issues from the perspective of her organizational role and to understand herself in the larger system.

While goals that might be more appropriate for personal analysis are not my focus, nor my area of expertise, I do believe that my client would greatly benefit from psychotherapy. What limited interest she has in working on her personal issues, however, is exclusively directed toward achieving success in her organization. One can presume that this is a client for whom psychotherapy might be overwhelming and anxiety arousing. I have had many clients who would greatly benefit from psychotherapy but feel safer exploring personal issues in the context of organizational ones. Leslie is a more extreme case, in that even face to face consultation seems to arouse unbearable anxiety in her. For someone like Leslie, who might not otherwise stay in consultation, I believe that working this way provides continuing connection and ultimately greater prospects for a better work life. Leslie does not have to disconnect to move forward nor does she have to be swamped by the other.

Given the unusual nature of this work, I have often reflected on why I undertook this consultation. I have been encouraged to continue by my client's commitment, my supervisor's help, my own economic gain, and my interest in exploring new territory.

As to the client herself, she is pleased with our work and often expresses her appreciation. From the perspective of her original goal, the consultation seems to be succeeding, as she has moved up the system impressively and now holds a senior position with her present company. As she has moved up in status and responsibility, I have experienced her to be less contemptuous of others and more professionally satisfied.

As has become evident, working by telephone dramatically influences how one consults. It requires a new learning curve. Without the visual and contextual clues characteristic of the preferred consulting situation, one must put greater emphasis on other sensibilities. The continuing question I ask is what is being excluded and what is being added by working this way. To continue to ask that question is to remain conscious of the ambivalent nature of this way of working and my own struggles to expand my insight and competency.

CHAPTER EIGHT

Drawing from role biography in Organizational Role Analysis

Susan Long

When we take up and engage a particular work role it is always in the context of a larger work system. The value of conceptualizing work systems as systems of role relations is that it emphasizes the interactions between roles and their links to the tasks of the enterprise. In contrast, the idea of "person" seems to have lost the essence of interaction or embeddedness in the system. Persons are often thought of as independent units in our increasingly individualistic and narcissistic society.

Role is at the intersection of the person and the system. Although a role is a structural part of the system, it is filled and shaped by its incumbent, the person. This person has a history of taking up different roles in different systems: family, community and work.

Many executive coaches focus solely on the person, aiding them to develop personal skills and capabilities that will help them in their roles. Organizational Role Analysis (ORA) or socio-analytic role consultation as discussed in this book looks also at the organization or system. There are mutual interactions, influences, and interconnections between the role of the client or person, other roles, and other organizational structures. Although individual role analysis typically encounters the system through the perceptions,

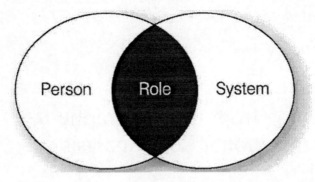

Figure 1. Person, role and system (Sievers, Workshop in London, 2000).

thoughts, and fantasies of the role holder (see Sievers & Beumer, this volume), when conducted in conjunction with organization culture analysis or research (Long, Newton, & Chapman, this volume) the organization-in-the-experience of the consultant/researcher and other players may also be examined. A broad picture of multiple representations requiring negotiation and mutual exploration arises. Each requires exploration if the dynamics of the client role are to be fathomed.

In this chapter, I discuss the idea of "role biography". I use this term to describe a biography of the *person-in-role* as described through the various work roles that they have taken up throughout their lives. I distinguish this from "role history", which is a history of a particular organizational role, shaped over time by its incumbents. Perhaps I have named these two terms rather arbitrarily, but the distinction is valid.

In role consultation I might explore both role biography and role history with the client. In their current work role, the client is at the intersection of their own role biography with the history of that role. This is always a unique position. Influences on the person in their current role come from both (i) the organization/system, the role history and its relatedness to other roles, and (ii) the person, their role biography, and their skills and attributes.

Role biography

I began working with role biographies as part of an induction workshop conducted for incoming management students as part of

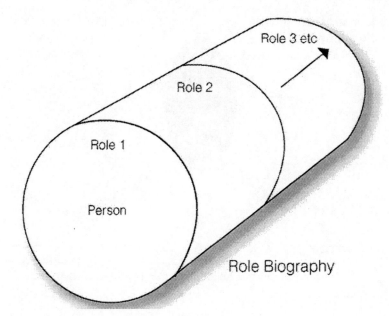

Figure 2.   Role biography.

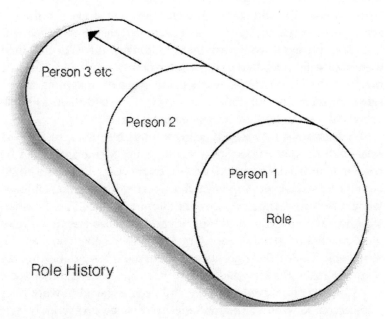

Figure 3.   Role history.

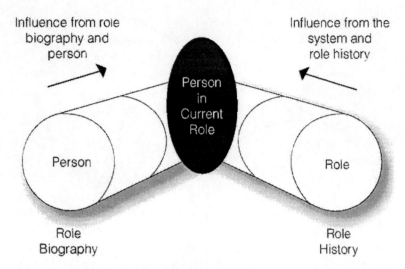

Influence from role
biography and
person

Influence from the
system and
role history

Person
in
Current
Role

Person

Role

Role
Biography

Role
History

Figure 4.   Influences from role biography and role history on the person in current role.

their university programme. It was a way of helping them understand each other's backgrounds. I would ask students to imagine themselves at different stages of their lives: first at age six, then at age sixteen, then at the age when they entered their first permanent job. At each stage I would ask them to think of the roles that they were taking up in relation to tasks in the family, at school, or in their neighbourhood. When we reached the stage of imagining themselves in their first full-time employment, I asked them to think about the work roles they had taken up there.

For each stage they would be given time to explore the recalled roles with another student or a small group. Memories would be revived that had not been accessed for many years. Examples might be of tasks such as peeling vegetables, caring for younger siblings, feeding the cat, doing a paper-round, ironing for neighbours, creating and running a library among friends. But also emotional roles would be linked to these. For example, being the one who was reliable, being the reckless one, always looking out for mum, being the one who made the tea when others were upset, the studious one. The students discovered that they had been engaged in work roles with accompanying socio-emotional roles since a very early age. Exploring these memories with others was fun, often moving, and sometimes sad. The exercise was particularly illuminating when done with students from quite different national and ethnic backgrounds.

The final part of the exercise was to explore how the roles at each of these stages were linked to current work roles. Could they find a pattern in their role biographies? What were some of the common themes emerging? Were there large breaks in the patterns? What might these mean for their current work roles? This exercise has always led to engagement and learning for the students. It was a way of getting to know one another but also, a method for self-discovery.

A few years ago I began to put the ideas behind this exercise together with the role drawing exercise that I use as part of ORA. I have used drawings in my work for many years. In my career as child psychotherapist I used drawings alongside play therapy to help the child express his or her ideas and fantasies and to explore the more unconscious phantasies present for the child. Working with families, I often used drawings alongside family histories. When children and their parents draw together, their ways of interacting are illuminated and can be explored with them, as well as their understandings of family history. The drawing acts as a transitional object and facilitates communication. So working with role drawings seemed to me a natural way of co-exploring the work experience with my clients. Next, I began to think about getting clients to explore their role biographies through drawing.

The drawing and its exploration

I ask the client to do a drawing. They may have already done a work drawing following the instruction "draw yourself in role at work", or "draw your organization with your place in it", so they may be familiar with the kind of task proposed. For this drawing I say, "The role biography is an attempt to look at the various work roles you have had in your life. You may have had a great many roles. Don't try to fit them all in, just those that you feel are most important to you or that first come to mind. Some will seem more important than others, although you may wish just to note others. Try just to make the drawing as of a journey starting from the roles you took up in your family, through childhood, adolescence, young adulthood until now." The drawing takes longer than the usual work drawing because the client has to go back through many memories and depict each. Often I will ask my client to do this between sessions and we explore the drawing in the next session.

In using work drawings, I learned that the type of instruction given makes quite a difference to the type of drawing produced. As ORA or "Socio-Analytic Role Consultation" is a mutually collaborative exploration with the client, we might often explore what would be the best kind of drawing for the consultation at the time of the drawing. The instructions "draw yourself in role", "draw your experience at work", or "draw your organization and your place in it" aid the exploration of different facets of work experience.

So it is also with role biography. One can explore the experience in roles at different stages of life, self in role, or self in various organizations. I have tended to use "draw yourself in roles throughout your life" and have emphasized the idea of a journey. The journey encourages multiple depictions that aid a more detailed exploration rather than the client forming a general picture to represent the whole biography from the start. The detail often provides more space for the client to learn things about their role biography than those ideas they have pre-formulated into a composite image. I ask that childhood and adolescence are included and state that roles in the family and at school are important for us to explore. These are formative years for the development of things like work ethic, choice of vocation, emotional role development, leadership capacity, attitudes to authority, and capacities to represent others.

When exploring the role biography, it is important that the consultant refrains from making direct interpretations. The idea is for the client to present his or her drawing, responding to queries of clarification about the drawing. "What is this you are doing here?" or "What does this stand for?" Following clarification, both client and consultant may associate to the drawing, expressing what it reminds them about.

I have used this exercise also in the socio-analytic training programme through the former Australian Institute of Socio-Analysis and in classes in the Organization Dynamics programme at RMIT University. Here a small group of about four to six members takes on the task of exploring role biographies with students presenting their drawings in turn. If time and task boundaries are managed carefully, the associations of the small group members can be very helpful in identifying otherwise overlooked implications in the drawing.

Finally, if it has not already occurred, the client is asked to make connections between the various roles taken up throughout life. Importantly, I stress, "What is the link between this role and your current work role?" "What might we understand about your current work role in light of this previous role?" This discussion may include those roles now remembered but not initially depicted. In fact, the exercise often brings back memories of fogotten roles and these may be important for their place in the role biography and whether or not they fit patterns discerned in the process.

Some case material

Sandra

Sandra is an organization consultant who likes to work primarily as a coach. She did two drawings as part of a workshop that I conducted. The workshop, called "Working with Roles", had an experiential design and was conducted over three days. One part of the workshop involved members of small groups sharing role drawings and exploring implications derived from the drawings and the process. The first drawing, done on the first day, was of Sandra in her primary work role. The second drawing, done on the second day, was a role biography. She explored the drawings in some depth at the workshop. I followed this up with an interview four months later.

Sandra described this as "me in my business". She then went on to say that "the business is me". She saw her primary role in the business as engaging with the coaching task. She pointed out that she was happy (hence the big smile) and that the work involved lots of listening and talking (hence the big ears and mouth). The arrows around her head stood for incoming information. Other lines depict information going out. She felt surrounded by information coming in and out. She felt clear that her work was mainly "in the head"; that she worked to give her clients choices and options rather than

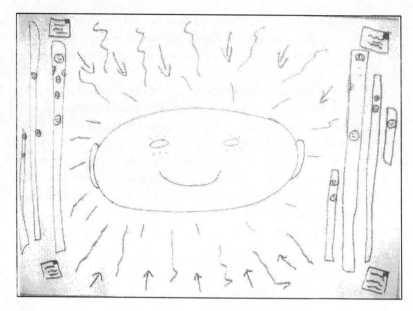

Figure 5. Sandra's drawing of her primary work role.

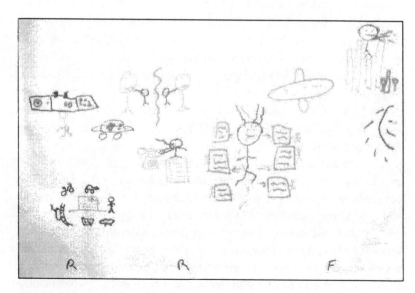

Figure 6. Sandra's role biography drawing.

her becoming involved in recommending action or becoming involved herself in action. The towers at the side of the drawing stood for the organizations she worked with. The faces in the towers depicted people at different organizational levels. She stressed her increasing understanding that she needed to work with those in senior levels if she were to influence practices in the organizations.

At each corner of the drawing are stamped envelopes. These, she said, represented the requirement for written work and documentation. For example, written reports for clients, business reports and taxation documentation, marketing materials, proposals, and invoices. She strongly disliked having to do this writing (hated it with a passion) and stressed that her preferred way of working was verbal. However, she recognized the increasing need for writing in her role. The letters in the drawing were placed so as to "frame" her other work. They also expressed a commitment to doing the writing, "without which my work would not occur".

As she explored this drawing, she expressed surprise at the size of the mouth she had drawn. She said that it was still a struggle for her to balance the amount of listening and talking that she had to do—what to hear and what to say. Her eyes, intended to look attentive, appeared to her now as excited. She was struck by the way the drawing showed clarity of purpose. The coaching role and herself as her business was central and focused. Later she said, "The drawing is all bliss, not a worry in the world. It shows me doing my core business [of coaching]. I enjoy it and am paid for it." She admitted that work was not "all bliss" though. Some things were hidden by the drawing.

Other complexities arose, however, when it came to the role biography drawing.

The role biography drawing roughly depicts four separate but connected sets of roles across time.

1. The family role and system.
On the lower left is a drawing of the things she liked when she was little. Important here was a train set. "Girls aren't supposed to like trains," she explained. But she still has this one. Above this on the upper left is a drawing of Sandra's role in her family of origin. There were four siblings in the family and they are drawn around the kitchen sink. Her role, along with the others, was to wash and

dry the family dishes after the evening meal. The social setting was one where chats, discussions, and arguments took place. Sandra particularly remembers engaging this role as a prelude to her "escape". In contrast to her siblings, she would spend much of her evening outside the family at friends' homes and then, when older, at other venues. She depicts herself as leaving the family home on foot, and later by car.

2. Adult family role and work role
The central part of the drawing is taken up by two pictures. The upper picture depicts Sandra in the middle of her two sisters, one older, the other, younger. These sisters would compete, especially over domestic tasks such as who was the best cook. Although alike, these sisters grew apart and Sandra found herself as a "go between and peacemaker", often representing one sister to the other or indirectly carrying messages between the two who would not approach each other directly. Sandra also often took on this role between her mother and sisters. The picture shows a dividing line between the sisters and Sandra as turning at one time to one, and another time to the other sister. As she described her drawing, she spoke of how she had finally realized the nature of the role she was playing and from then on refused to continue, telling her sisters and mother to engage each other directly. She believes she had taken up the role because "everything had been such a big deal to them and I became like two separate people in the discussion—one with each sister". This had left her feeling split.

Just below this is a depiction of Sandra's first major work role. Here, at age seventeen, she was "paid to sit on the phone talking to people and making appointments for them" with eight or so doctors in the public sector. She had got this job herself despite, or perhaps because of, her father's offer of finding her work at his place of employment. This job seemed to capitalize on her enjoyment of talking with people and her ability to be "in-between" others. She had wanted to leave school, feeling it was a "necessary evil", and eventually was expelled for misbehaviour. The one regret she had (saying this with some irony) was not paying attention in geography classes because later in life she travelled a lot but really didn't have a sense of where countries were in relation to one another. She later enrolled in a course in public administration.

The other central picture shows her as the National Human Resource Manager of a large organization that consisted in part of a group of laboratories. Their work was predominantly in drug testing associated with sport. Her work was mainly in restructuring and downsizing. This role had followed a series of roles in smaller organizations, first in administration, then moving to Human Resources. She had now worked her way into a bigger role that meant a lot of travel between locations throughout Australia. "I don't know how I did it sometimes," she said. "I was always on the go, away every week and organizing the travel myself. The General Manager was better off staying in Canberra, so I always offered to be the one who travelled. It was self-imposed. I had seen him strained by travel. One day I saw him in the airport stooping and looking old." So Sandra took over most of his travel to the sites. "When I left, they replaced me with three people," she said.

In this job the theme of helping also emerged. She was trying to help scientists move on in the face of the company restructure. This was difficult in the face of the scientists' attitudes that a "job was for life". For some people it took up to a year. She wanted to take care because the change was traumatic for some and there had been suicides in the history of the company. She helped over one hundred people to move on. She was once more in an "in-between" role. This was also evidenced in her getting in between the General Manager and the travel he was doing.

3. Current role

The last picture on the right is a partial reproduction of her first picture in miniature. She has moved to her own business, celebrating her success, but feels she is "not quite in it yet". The picture is half off the page. While talking about this part of the picture she began to realize that although she had wanted to create a business with coaching as its core, she had not yet achieved this. She was distracted into other work more than she felt she should be. She would often be drawn into work that she was offered rather than proactively seeking the work she wanted to form the core of her buisness.

Following the workshop she had thought a lot about the drawings, especially her half-formed business. At the interview she said that she now saw her business as having three tiers. The core was coaching work. The second tier was to do "one-on-one" work of a related nature, such as debriefings following management training programmes or feedback from exercises such as "360 degree" exercises where the direct reports, peers, and managers of a person in role are surveyed with respect to the person's work capabilities. The third tier was group work such as conflict resolution or team building. She liked this latter work the least. She realized that the roots to her preference for coaching lay in her biography; this was her preference. We discussed that it might be her "valency", to use Bion's (1961) term. Coaching can be seen as a helping role, but also as a role of being "in-between". The coach becomes a transitional object for the client while he or she is attempting to make changes to their own work roles.

Currently she is working with a coach to explore her own role. She has taken her drawings from the workshop to this coach and believes they help the work she is doing there. In particular, she is working on marketing and a business plan. "I had quite a shock in the workshop when I saw how my business was half off the page. I never before thought that I might have to do a lot more thinking about how to set up my business, especially in terms of driving my own focus, but doing the drawings brought this to light."

Cheryl

Cheryl is a medical doctor who works in the emergency department of a general hospital. She did two role biography drawings nearly two years apart in two different programmes. Although the two drawings are similar, she felt that the second one reflected more complexity. In the time between the two drawings she had done intensive experiential learning in socio-analysis. The discussion reported in this paper took place some months after the second drawing had been done and shows how role biography drawings can also be used at a later date than when they are first drawn. It seems from the work with Cheryl that new information and learning can come on returning to the drawings. Cheryl could broadly remember her initial associations to the drawing, but also used the time with me to make current associations. She first explained the meaning of the drawing to me and then added her current reflections.

Figure 7.

FIRST DRAWING (FIGURE 7)

Cheryl drew an ear, an eye, and a heart to begin her role biography. These were to become a strong motif throughout the drawings. She said that as a baby and small child she took on the role of hearing and seeing and feeling the tears in the family. "That is how I've learned and how I work," she explained. She believes that her sensitivity to feelings was an important ingredient in her becoming a doctor and working with the suffering of others.

As she grew, she also took on more practical roles. These are represented by the broom and the ironing board. But the practical roles were aimed at "smoothing things out; keeping things clean and tidy; working out problems".

In the centre of the picture she represents her "fantasy roles". She took ballet lessons and played the piano. She also imagined herself as an opera singer. Among these is a drawing of herself as a doctor. "I was very young when I decided to be a doctor", she explained, "perhaps six or seven." There had been a doctor who visited her home while they were living in the country and she had been very impressed by him. In her fantasy picture she holds a stethoscope to her own heart, indicating her passion for medicine. At the left of these representations she depicts herself playing with other children. Play was "off to the side". She spent more time on her own with her imaginings and fantasies than playing with the others.

To the right of the picture are two more sets of ear, eye, and heart. These she felt permeated her work life as an adult. Her work involves her in seeing and hearing patients and their problems, but also involves her feelings and how she uses them in her work. A picture of the world appears at the top right hand side of the drawing. On looking at this she saw it as a "female in the world". The globe is drawn as the female sign. It also represents her as a team player. She explained that she played a lot of sport as a teenager and young adult. Now she feels what she learned and experienced then is related to her capacity to be part of a medical team.

Having explained the drawing she studied it as a whole. Her first comment was that she was surprised that there were no books in the drawing. Her studies had taken a great deal of time in her life, yet she hadn't represented them. She then looked at the lower right hand section of the drawing and noted that she had drawn a "heart within a heart". She recognized how much the drawing was representing pain, beauty, joy, and tears. Although her work involves having to use her intellect she recognized how much she uses her "heart first—learning at the heart level and using my head to interpret later".

THE SECOND DRAWING (FIGURE 8)

This drawing was done about four months prior to our discussion. On the upper left hand side the biography begins with hearing, seeing, and feeling. But in this drawing, the eyes are looking inward more than outward. This time there are no tears.

As with the first drawing, she goes on to draw the practical work she did in the family. Once more there is the broom and the cleaning. This time cooking is added, and a tea-towel with a cup and saucer. Behind this, faintly drawn, is a large hand.

Just to the right of this are depictions of a ball, a figure at a desk at school, a piano, and lots of small figures actively running around playing sport. On looking at the drawing she reflected "It's as though I've taken up quite different roles with different parts of myself. First the seeing, hearing, and feeling, next I'm used as a helper with my hands and my strength. In the next part I'm using

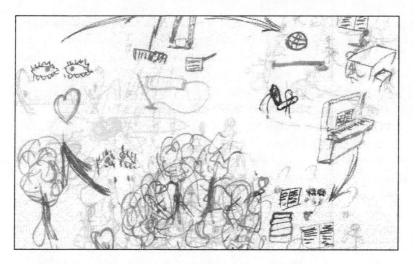

Figure 8.

my feet in team sports and then finally my brain at school in my studies."

The bottom right hand part of the picture shows her life as a medical student. Here we see the books, the study, and the first depiction of the doctor with eyes, ears, heart, and a stethoscope. There are question marks around the students, indicating her questioning of herself as a scholar. The doctor as helper is at the centre of this cluster of drawings at this stage of her life. She felt that there was a "simplicity around life as a student". Her parents bought a house in the city and she lived there some of the time and away from home, alone, some of the time.

The section at the bottom centre of the drawing is a complex series of trees, figures, lines, hearts, and swirls. She represents sad eyes looking inward, bright light, sunshine and flowers, a stethoscope listening to a heart. It is a mixture of sadness at the suffering in the world and hope and joy in looking at growth. This represents the time in her life when there were "many questions, growth, and lots of people". A strong purple feminist arrow leads out of this back to her heart.

She then looked at the whole picture. "I see so much sadness, trauma, and pain in my work," she said. In this picture the eyes are turning inward and don't have tears like they had in the first picture. "Sometimes tears are not an acceptable way of connecting."

She spoke of how in her work she had to maintain professionalism and balance this against her feelings, although they were always there. She noted that the second picture had less of what she had called the "fantasy part" than the first. With some regret she talked of the intensity of her work, leaving little space to be fanciful. "Someone else will play the pianola." She also noted that in the second picture she was the doctor. In the first she was the fantasy doctor of her childhood.

I asked her what she had gained through the drawing process. She said that she now had a greater sense of "who I am in my work and how I became who I am. It opened up that". She mused, "it's a privilege to have this sort of background that's exposed me to heartfelt knowledge". She remembered again the doctor who had come to her house when she was small. "There was pain in the house. The doctor came and made things better. I wanted to do that." She said that the drawings had brought back memories and that she had not put them all together in this way before.

It seemed to me that Cheryl had integrated her early experience in her family and the roles she had taken there into her current work role as an emergency physician. The motif of eyes, ears, and heart expressed the way that she had combined intellectual and emotional capacities. Cheryl had told me that she always felt different from other children and had taken the emotional pain of her family into herself. This became focused as a vocation when she met the doctor who had helped her family. Much of her medical training had emphasized a more distant, clinical approach to patients than she was able to feel. However, she is able to accept her own approach and sensitivity to patients in the emergency ward as an important part of the psychological as well as the physical healing process. Understanding the role she plays within the medical system and its roots in the family system has helped her to more readily use her psychological sensitivity professionally.

Conclusion

Role biography provides a method for understanding the impact of various roles taken throughout life on the client's current work role. This can give the role holder a better sense of his or her uniqueness in role. It can also give a fuller understanding of where valencies in role have their origins. New roles are not taken up in a vacuum. The person has a history of role taking.

Exploring role biography requires an openness to the meanings that might emerge by both client and consultant. Interpretations made early in the process, or from the consultant rather than the client, may inhibit this, or worse still, lead to "wild analysis". The use of working hypotheses (Lawrence, this volume) is needed. The consultant should be trained in systems psychodynamic (socio-analytic) methods where sensitive listening, an understanding of countertransference, and the use of reflective space are emphasized. This is because a major way the role biography works is through the client's coming to explore, make conscious, and understand their own transferences from role to role. The whole process requires an empathetic setting where the work of formulating working hypotheses is valued. Although, with time, it allows for many stories to emerge and is akin to the narrative psycho-social interview method described by Hollway and Jefferson (2000), as with their method, the work involves more than giving a voice to the client. The collaborative development of working hypotheses allows meaning to emerge. The stories become interrelated and linked to current work issues and provide a context for their exploration.

Moreover, when people from the same workplace explore role biographies together, there grows a deeper understanding of why particular role holders approach mutual tasks in the way they do. The role biography process opens a space for re-negotiation of role boundaries and for dialogue. I think this is because, while everyone has different role ideas (in-the-mind and in-experience) about their own and others' roles, the role biography exploration allows for the emergence of explanations about how these ideas originate. The "rightness" or "wrongness" about role is subsumed by questions of how it is that a particular role becomes shaped as it does, given the person, their role biography, and the role history in the system.

The concepts of role biography and role history set the constellation of person–role–system in a yet even broader context: that of time.

CHAPTER NINE

Coaching senior executives: personal/work conflicts, mortality, and legacy

Laurence J. Gould

Introduction

While both the study of life stages and the nature of taking up an organizational role have been the subject of much contemporary work, with few exceptions (e.g., Fitzgerald, 2002; Gould, 1999; Levinson, Darrow, Klein, Levinson, & McKee, 1978), they have generally been split into personal and professional strands, with little in the way of systematic integration. For example, the literature on coaching most often mentions the significance of life stages only in passing, or not at all. Even, in what is an excellent paper by Brunning (2001), in which she conceptualizes, quite comprehensively, six major domains of coaching and applies them to a well-developed case example, she never mentions the client's age. This, despite the fact, that one of her domains—the "Life Story"—is at least suggestive in this regard. As a general matter, I can hardly imagine that one wouldn't view the case material somewhat differently, nor that a client's concerns would be likely to be quite different, depending on their stage of life. But this example is hardly unique—it is representative of the mainstream literature on coaching.

Therefore, by way of exemplifying a life stage perspective, I will attempt to bring to the fore some of the normative issues that many experience, as they relate to the demands and psychological needs of being an organizational "senior". At best, while "senior" is a somewhat arbitrary concept, and it is fruitless to try to define it with any precision, I am going to use two broad criteria to circumscribe the domain I wish to address—the *late adulthood*[1] stage of life as defined by Levinson, Darrow, Klein, Levinson, and McKee (1978), and the nature of the senior executive role in the organization. With regard to the former, the evidence (e.g., Karp, 1988; Levinson, 1996;[2] Levinson, Darrow, Klein, Levinson, & McKee, 1978;) suggests that reminders of mortality consciously begin to emerge in the mid fifties, and continue until the end of one's personal and organizational work life and, as such, represent the initiation of the senior stage of life. As for the latter, I wish to focus on those men and women whose senior executive leadership roles carry sufficient authority potentially to have a significant impact on their organizations' functioning and future.

Becoming a senior

While, on one level, becoming an organizational senior represents for most, a positive affirmation and culmination of a successful career, it also often brings with it a considerable increase in demands and responsibilities. Further, as I indicated above, many theorists have noted that the fifties and beyond also signal the beginning of a major life transition, and not uncommonly the activation of powerful psychological forces, conflicts, and dilemmas. The major task and emotional challenge of this transition is that of beginning the process of preparing for the last phase of life, in all domains, including, of course, one's organizational work roles. Specifically, it is during this time[3] that, for many, with the end of one's career in sight, and mortality beginning to peep over the horizon, a major transformation of self-in-world occurs. This usually includes a reassessment of values, relationships, and role choices or modifications, as well as an assessment of dreams fulfilled and unfulfilled, and as such, it is a time when concerns about one's personal, social, and organizational legacies begin to emerge at the forefront of consciousness. In the context of these concerns, a critical issue is: how does being a senior shape the ways in which they take up their organizational roles, and how do they think and feel generally about their work lives, as it relates to their life as a whole? I suggest that struggling with such issues, consciously and unconsciously, is the norm at this stage.

Context: some notes on the life cycle and a conception of adult development

To provide a general overview of life stages and a theory of adult development, I draw most heavily on the first major research study of Levinson and his colleagues (1978). As they conceptualize it, adult development is best characterized as the evolution of the *individual life structure*. Their research suggests that the life structure neither remains static, nor does it change adventitiously. Rather, they argue, it goes through a sequence of *eras* that last roughly eighteen to twenty years (*early adulthood, middle adulthood, late adulthood, and late, late adulthood*), and that within these *eras* a sequence of *stable* and *transitional periods* alternate. The *stable periods* ordinarily last for approximately six to eight years, and the *transitional periods* from four to five years

Further, they argue that the evolution of the life structure, during any given developmental period—stable or transitional—is defined in terms of its major primary tasks. Specifically, they note that

> the primary (developmental) task of [a] stable period is to build a life structure (whatever content or substance it may have). This process involves making certain key choices, forming a structure around them, and pursuing desired goals and values within this structure [*ibid.*, p. 49]

While many changes may occur during any given stable period, they argue that the basic underlying life structure remains relatively intact. They go on to note that

> the primary tasks of [a] transitional period, by contrast, are to question and reappraise an existing structure, to explore the various

possibilities for change of self-in-world, and to make the crucial
choices that will form the basis of a new life structure in the ensuing stable period [*ibid.*, p. 49]

Three aspects of Levinson's conception of adult development
need be highlighted in order to make the ensuing discussion meaningful. First, it is an age–stage model. That is, not only does it postu-
late a predictable developmental sequence for the adult life course,
but also a normative time frame for each period.[4] Second, the model
places a particular emphasis on the nature of an individual's *dream*,[5]
or its absence, in shaping the quality and character of development.
And third, the concept of the *individual life structure* refers to the
patterning or design of the individual's life at a given time—
defined in the broadest terms as one's sense of self-in-the-world.
That is, the substance and texture of one's engagement with their
family, social networks, organizations, and society.

The case

Introduction

To illustrate the ideas outlined above, I offer a coaching case with a
senior executive, and attempt, given my experience with many
other similar coaching engagements, to outline some general issues
that seem representative of, and critical for ones' effectiveness in
working with clients during this stage of life. After presenting the
case material, I'll return to a consideration of these issues, and how
they may inform the coaching process when working with this
group. My explicit aim in doing so is to selectively restrict what I
have to say about the role dilemmas of such clients and the issues
that emerge in coping with them at their particular stage of life,
without any implication that many other aspects of coaching are
less important.

FIRST SESSION

A sixty-one-year-old lawyer—John Samuals—was referred to me by his
analyst to help him sort out some work-related and career issues that
he was in an increasing quandary about. He was a man who had a

quite successful career, and at the point at which we met he was the managing partner of a large, prestigious law firm. He had occupied that role for six years.

His initial presentation was what one might anticipate, given his position and the prominence of his firm. He met me with a firm handshake, was seemingly in excellent physical health, well dressed, direct, and quite adroit interpersonally. With virtually no prompting he articulately told me about his situation, and the dilemmas he was struggling with, and why his analyst felt that coming to me for coaching might be useful. However, I was most struck by the quality and appraisal of his situation—thoughtful, psychologically-minded and perceptive—as if it was all quite well understood. Perhaps this was not surprising, especially since he was in analysis, where it was likely that he had many opportunities to discuss his situation, as he initially presented it to me.

My immediate reactions were that he was a quite likeable and appealing man, whose presentation was easy and effortless to take in. However, throughout his account, I had the persistent feeling that it was so complete and seamless that I wondered if I had anything to contribute that couldn't usefully be taken up in his treatment. Clearly, he and his analyst had done considerable work on the issues he was grappling with. I raised this with him, and asked what additional insight or assistance he thought I could offer him, rather than simply continuing to work on his concerns in treatment. He was a bit unsettled by this question, and obviously did not have a "smooth" answer. He first suggested that he hadn't given it much thought, and that, having high regard for his analyst, did not question the reason for the referral in any detail. I then asked him what his thoughts and associations about it were at the moment. After a brief silence, he said "I felt immediately comfortable that you were about my age[6] and not"—he hesitated here, and continued with an awkward chuckle—"a youngster like my analyst."[7] He went on to say that he felt surprised that he called his analyst a "youngster", even though he had thought about him that way before. But he was clearly put off stride by this exchange, and it felt to me as if his confident, initial presentation started to visibly crumble somewhat before my eyes.

I shared my experience with him, and asked why he thought that the turn the discussion had taken, and his remark about his analyst, had made him uncomfortable. He responded by saying that I was correct in noticing his discomfort, and that his analyst's age had, in fact, been on his mind at times, but that he had never brought it up with him, although he didn't have any idea why. I suggested that he may have felt some sense of shame or humiliation that he needed help, especially from a younger man. He thought that perhaps this was the case, but did not recall this particular thought ever having entered his mind. I changed the subject and then asked whether he thought that there were any connections between his feelings about his age, and the work dilemma he initially described as the source of his distress.

This direct and obvious question had a powerful impact on him, and in both demeanour and verbally he indicated that he imagined it had everything to do with it. He then, in a rush of words, told me that among other aspects of his life, his father had died at the age of sixty-three, and that he really didn't know what he wanted at this point in his life, nor for that matter, in the future. And, he added, "to make matters worse, if I were to do anything different, or make any change at all, would I have the time to do it?" I asked him if he could be more specific, since I wasn't sure what the "anything" or the "it" referred to, and whether these thoughts and feelings only applied to his work. Once again, he became visibly uncomfortable, but at this point the session was at an end. He then, immediately took out his date book, and asked when we could meet again. I said that I thought it would make more sense to discuss our meeting with his analyst, before making any decision as to whether there was something to be gained by seeing me that he couldn't just as well work on in his treatment. He assented quickly, but with little conviction, and seemed quite unhappy that I didn't immediately agree to our setting up another appointment. I added that, if in discussing it with his analyst, it seemed to make sense for us to meet again, to give me a call.

THE WORK CONTINUES: SESSION TWO

About a week later John called and left a message that, as I had suggested, he discussed the situation with his analyst, and they agreed that it would be useful for him to continue his coaching work with me. At the beginning of the session, when we next met, I inquired, in detail, about his discussion with his analyst and the basis for the decision. He said that his analyst felt that I could add a dimension to his concerns about the relationship between his age and his work situation, while his feelings about his age *per se*, personal concerns about his future, and the significance of the differences in their ages could be worked on in treatment. I provisionally took this view at face value, but I also had the anxious feeling, from the way he reported this, that his analyst may have felt uncomfortable by my introducing age as an important element into the treatment, which he had either neglected, or had gone unnoticed. My unease further increased at this point, in that I distinctly felt that John had developed an immediate, strong positive transference to me, and I worried about how this might affect his treatment.[8]

THE REMAINING THREE SESSIONS: AN OVERVIEW

What initially emerged quite rapidly in the subsequent sessions was an elaboration of his presenting issue: John was torn between remaining the firm's managing partner, a role in which he was quite competent, or returning to the practice of law, in which he had also been quite successful. As he experienced it, he was torn between an obligation to the firm, and pursuing his personal desires. In connection with the former, he had become the managing partner during a time of considerable turmoil and discontent, and was asked to assume this role by his senior colleagues, who felt he had the respect, wisdom, and temperament to restore the firm to a state of emotional and professional well-being. As it transpired, he accomplished this task in fairly short order, and discovered in the process that he had both an interest in, and talent for, leadership and management. However, now some six years later, with the firm on a solid footing, he questioned whether it made sense for him to step down. On one side, he felt that while he had been able to manage the serious rifts in the firm that originally led to his being asked to take on the managing partner role, he worried that if he stepped down they would again erupt. On the other, he felt that the rifts had been sufficiently healed, and that several of his senior partners could easily take the helm. Was this latter view an accurate appraisal, he wondered out loud, or a self-serving justification for wanting to relinquish the managing partner role? He had gone back and forth incessantly on this issue in the past several months, but still felt that he could not be certain.

As his story unfolded, he first described a concern about his institutional legacy—a well run, prosperous, and admired firm, for which he was publicly acknowledged, both by his colleagues and the profession at large, as having been the major architect. But, he also increasingly felt that, while the major challenges were behind him, if he stepped down as managing partner his contribution to saving the firm would soon be forgotten, or worse yet, as noted, that the firm would again go into decline without his steady hand to guide it. He then elaborated by telling me about several other kinds of feelings he had about staying in this role: that at the end of even a good, productive day he experienced little in the way of enduring satisfaction. He said he often had the sense that he was just pushing pieces of paper around, and felt more and more peripheral. He continued by saying, quite forcefully, "The action is in doing the work." In comparing his managerial role to that of practising law, he asked me if I ever heard the expression in the *Talmud* to the effect that "If you save but one person you save the world". He felt that, at its best, this is what the practice of law offered, but being a manager didn't. This was an obvious variation of the cliché that "those who can do, and those who can't teach". He also told me that his wife often reminded him, when they discussed this, how much more stress he had experienced when he was in practice, and that perhaps he was now idealizing it, feeling somewhat unfulfilled in his present role.

After quite a few discussions, working with this formulation of his dilemma, he seemed to become quite depressed. When I inquired about this he said that he had begun to feel a desperate need to set things right, to think well of himself, and to be remembered well by others with whom he was close. Listening to his concerns I felt they were, in part, driven by guilt, and a painful sense of self-recrimination that he hadn't quite lived up to his *ego ideal*[9] - a not unusual reparative urge at this stage of life, when one feels the press of time to heal one's sense of integrity (Erikson, 1985) and to "balance" accounts. However natural such feelings may be, they were acutely painful for John. While, currently, his life was satisfactory on the surface—and certainly to the outside world—he had gone into analysis because he felt increasingly depressed that he was repeating some of the same destructive patterns with his present wife that had resulted in a painful, failed relationship with his first wife. He further told me that a major unresolved source of distress and concern was a long-standing, tempestuous relationship with his two children (from his first marriage), both of whom were now in their mid/late thirties.

With this material now centre stage, I suggested that perhaps he had been trying to come to grips with some central issues in his life by both constricting them and splitting them off, without awareness, into his manifest work-related quandary, which served the function of covering over, or keeping an emotional distance from, the deeper concerns that had led him to seek analysis. I further elaborated by noting that I was struck, not as much with the content of his work quandary, as with the extent and quality of his obsessional preoccupation with it. I suggested that, given how lumbered he was with so many other significant life issues that had emerged in our meetings, perhaps his not being able to resolve his work dilemma might be viewed as a barrier against experiencing fully and struggling with his other, deeper concerns.

In light of this, I asked him which of the career choices he was trying to decide about might be more consonant with what he wanted to accomplish at this point in his life, given the considerations noted above. I suggested that linking them might provide a more useful basis for deciding. His response had the quality of a switch being thrown. He said, almost immediately, that the choice was clear—he would return to the practice of law rather than remaining in the Managing Partner role. He then said "It's simple—if I remain the Managing Partner, although it is no longer either particularly demanding or challenging, it does require me to be around and 'on call' a great deal. On the other hand, aside from the excitement of practising law again, which I miss, even though it was, as my wife reminded me, quite stressful, I can easily cut down on my practice at this point, leaving me more time to work on being with my wife and children in a different way, which is a hell of a lot more important." "I also think", he added as a postscript, "that I would not find practice as stressful at this point in my life as I had earlier on." He went on to to say that it was now clear he could find greater satisfaction both at work and at home, without sacrificing one for the other.

On this note, I urged him to bring these insights back to his treatment. He replied that "it had made the obvious, obvious, . . . it helped me get clear about my difficulties, and how they are connected to my work stuff, and although obvious now, I was too blocked and anxious to make these connections myself." I replied that it was commonly the case that anxiety often constricted a person's ability to think more broadly about the issues they are struggling with, which he was now able to do, and concluded that beyond this, I felt there was little else that any further coaching might offer him at this time. He reluctantly agreed, saying that our discussions had been extremely helpful, but asked if he could meet with me in the future if he felt it would be of benefit. I said we could certainly discuss this, if and when the occasion arose.[10]

Discussion and summary

Although it would be quite easy to provide additional, detailed material, I hope that the hypothesis I initially offered, to the effect that there is an intimate link between how one conceives and experiences one's role, and how it unfolds during a particular stage of life, is made clear by this case, and how critical this perspective is for the work of coaching.

In outline, by way of an example, my hypothesis can further be elaborated by noting what I believe is a useful distinction between coaching senior executives on the early side of seniorhood, and those on the later side. This is not, of course, a dichotomous distinction between categories, but rather a continuum on which the issues and their relative importance shift as one moves from the earlier to the later stage. For the purposes of exposition, however, I will discuss these separately, but focus on the themes of later seniorhood in greater detail.

Early seniorhood (from approximately the early/mid fifties to the late fifties)

On the earlier side, the issues senior executives often present tend to focus on a concern about their "final" organizational position. The question for them is whether they feel that their ambitions and dreams have been fulfilled—e.g., to head the most prestigious division of their organization, to become a CEO, or the CEO of a larger enterprise, etc.—and whether they will be able to attain it. The coaching task in such instances has less to do with working with them on their organizational roles *per se*, than in helping them to think about the meaning of their aspirations for the desired culmination of their careers. In such situations, coaching essentially takes the form of a career consultation, rather than an exploration of the dilemmas in the roles they currently occupy, except in so far as they believe that how they perform in them will potentially optimize the likelihood of achieving their desired goals.

Later seniorhood (from approximately the late fifties to the late sixties)

The role dilemmas many older executives present, intertwined as they are with the personal issues of coming to terms with the scope and trajectory of all facets of their adult lives as the end approaches, are often much more poignant and painful. To engage with them on these issues is, therefore, a necessity, however one may do so; conversely, neglecting them is, at best, virtually to miss the central aspect of working with this group, or at worst, to collude with strengthening a defensive, covering-over solution that may have far reaching consequences: that at a critical juncture in their lives, further development may well be inhibited, with the likelihood that hopelessness and despair will increasingly triumph over integrity as the end approaches (Erikson, 1985).[11]

In sum, the major challenge for senior executives at this stage, who must begin to prepare for the finality of their lives, is that of finding or creating solutions more consonant and congruent with emerging desires, guiding ideals, and developmentally appropriate needs. These may include a renewed wish for personal fulfillment, the pursuit of cherished activities and interests left behind in the climb up the organizational ladder, and, perhaps most important of all, struggling with and confronting the personal aspects of one's legacy in life, related to, but only an aspect of, one's career legacy.[12] These needs, for example, may include making reparation for past injustices, for the reconciliation and the repair of damaged relationships, reconnecting with significant others, whom they may have left behind, and working to insure the continuity, viability, and future of their families.

Finally, the material above raises, at least by implication, some critical questions about the nature of coaching altogether. Although it is beyond the scope of this chapter to discuss these in any detail, a central question, I believe, is worth noting. Specifically, it is how one defines the nature of coaching in the first place, with a central dimension being whether it is defined in a more restricted and circumscribed way, or more broadly and inclusively. That is, those holding to the former view may define coaching as focusing almost exclusively on the client's role, and the dilemmas he/she has in taking it up, with the goal of achieving greater effectiveness within it. On the other hand, those holding the latter view may feel quite comfortable including a counselling, therapeutic, and/or a career development dimension as an aspect of their coaching work. As such, the activities engaged in by the different coaches may vary considerably (even among those sharing a similar orientation!). But given the ostensible, major differences in these respective orientations, especially at the extremes, those with a more restrictive view tend to consider an inclusive definition as a serious distortion of what they consider the appropriate nature of the coaching process and its boundaries, clearly distinguishing it from counselling, therapeutic, or career interventions.[13] Others though, who operate with a more inclusive perspective, tend to view these activities not only as seamless, but with the exception of clients having serious emotional difficulties, more useful than arbitrarily separating them. But this distinction is hardly a firm one. In practice, there is a considerable grey area between these respective views, and much overlap.

In conclusion, it is worth emphasizing that much more often than not, it is my experience that a great majority of coaching engagements with senior executives—to the detriment of both the individual and the organization—do not systematically include an exploration of the deep emotional concerns that many may have about the conjunction of their work, personal, and family legacies, as mortality increasingly becomes an ever-present companion.[14] Therefore, if coaching at this stage of life is to have any serious and enduring transformative potential, such neglect, if valid, as I believe it is, warrants serious consideration and a need to understand the reasons for it more fully.[15]

Notes

1. When I first introduce them, I italicize those concepts and life stage descriptors used by Levinson, Darrow, Klein, Levinson, and McKee (1978).

2. Except where quoted, all future references to Levinson refer interchangeably to these two volumes. The first (1978), documents his research on the male life cycle, and the second (1996) on the female life cycle.

3. While it is not unusual in the contemporary work world that one can become an organizational senior at a much earlier age, this is not the group that I focus on. The reason is easy to state: becoming a senior at an earlier age likely stimulates a quite different constellation of concerns, dilemmas, and anxieties.

4. Levinson's overall life stage model is not simply a theory. It represents the empirical findings of his research. The same holds for his conception of the *Dream*, and that of the *individual life structure*.

5. Influenced by Jung (1971), the concept of the *Dream* is defined by Levinson, Darrow, Klein, Levinson, and McKee (1978) as follows: "In its primordial form, the Dream is a vague sense of self-in-adult world.

It has the quality of a vision, an imagined possibility that generates excitement and vitality. . . . It makes a great difference in growth whether . . . the life structure is consonant and infused by the *Dream*, or opposed to it. If the Dream remains unconnected to [ones'] life it may simply die, and with it [a] sense of aliveness and purpose (pp. 91, 92)."

6. I am sixty seven, and his analyst was forty five.

7. This exchange suggests how feelings about the respective ages of the client and coach, whatever they may be—similar to that of a therapist and patient—are a a significant aspect of the relationship, which needs to be fully explored.

8. In such situations, a common concern relates to splitting the transference, and thus attenuating it. Further, since coaching generally is a considerably more interactive process, with a more restricted focus than psychoanalysis or psychoanalytically-informed psychotherapy, some clients may come to feel that they are getting more direct benefit from coaching than from their treatment.

9. To condense and paraphrase the essential aspect of Freud's (1914) notion of the ego ideal, it can be defined as one's ideal concept of the self.

10. In this connection it is easy to understand the cautions indicated in note number nine. His case is a good example, in that his very positive transference to me would, if we continued, negatively affect his treatment. If he weren't in therapy, I probably would have either renegotiated my contract with him from that of a coaching to a therapeutic relationship—conceptualizing the sessions we had had as an extended consultation—or made an appropriate referral,

11. In his description of the eighth and final stage of ego development—*integrity* vs. *despair*—Erikson (1985) notes that there is a need at this stage for "a meaningful interplay between beginning and end, as well as some finite sense of summary, and possibly, a more active anticipation of dying" (p. 63). In his view, *wisdom* will be the emergent "virtue" if development is felicitous, and *despair* if it is not.

12. I have purposely not taken up the issue of succession, and its relation to feelings one may have about their legacy, important though it may be. Since the circumstances, context, and meaning in which it occurs is so varied, it is difficult to offer any useful generalizations. In many organizations, for example, senior executives—especially CEOs—may have a significant role and investment in choosing their successors, but in others, they may, by design, be entirely excluded from the process. However, a very common, and notably painful exception is the issue of

succession in family businesses. Whatever the formal succession arrangements may be to pass the leadership role on to the next generation, it is commonly quite problematic psychologically (especially if it is the second generation in the business). Much more often than not, the founding patriarch/matriarch continues to exert a powerful influence on the business, often to the detriment of the successor son's or daughter's ability to lead effectively, and as such, may potentially result in painful conflicts, creating serious tensions in the family as a whole.

13. For an excellent, detailed discussion of these issues, especially the relationship between psychotherapy and coaching, see White (2001). Also, Brunning's (2001) general perspective about the nature of coaching, and her specific comments about this issue are quite apposite.

14. While the experiences and dilemmas I've described are, in my experience, very common, I do not wish to suggest that the for the majority, or even for many senior executives, this stage of life and work is necessarily a time of great pain, turmoil or crisis. For a great many, the transitional process, although it involves potent emotional issues, may be quite benign, and experienced as a relatively uncomplicated unfolding of their lives.

15. I believe that one obvious candidate is the coach's own anxieties about aging and mortality, either with regard to themselves or ageing parents, the particular's depending on their own stage of life.

CHAPTER TEN

Organizational Role Analysis in management education

John Newton

The space to be filled is the difference between the established educational provision for managers, based upon what is believed to be required or what is marketable, and what is emerging from research as the reality of management. A necessary competence in analytic skills and techniques does nothing to encourage a reflective understanding of the complexities and nuances of organizational relationships and distributed power, not does it do much to develop a critical response to the vagaries of organizational and personal authority. Perhaps it is the needs of teachers rather than managers that have encouraged a concentration on the strict mechanisms of rational bureaucracy instead of the uncertainties and subtleties of negotiated order

(Reed & Anthony, 1992, p. 56)

My interest in the subject of this book held no particular label when I first became concerned about helping managers to deal with the multiple pressures they experienced in their work. As it happened, during the early 1980s my academic appointment in a School of Business involved me both in teaching Organization Behaviour to postgraduate management students and consulting to large Australian corporations. These consulting assignments derived from my reputation as an innovative teacher of management students who made good use of "experiential" methods; these assignments often involved the design and delivery of in-house management development programmes.

At the university I worked with a small group of academic colleagues, all of whom had industry experience, and who were much taken with an experiential approach to teaching and leaning that drew principally from the work of Kolb (1984), Revans (1983), and the T-group tradition. Our reputation for a student (client)-centred stance brought invitations from corporations seeking to revitalize their development programmes for middle to senior managers. Typically, these programmes were of one to two weeks duration and involved participants who had been nominated by someone "higher-up" in the organization. The programmes were a mix of on-site and off-site activities designed primarily to develop the managerial skills deemed necessary to implement the strategic decisions being made at the executive level. In retrospect, it seems significant that, despite my espoused stance of being client-centred, these programmes were usually structured around topics that were framed by programme sponsors: topics such as leadership, communication skills, negotiating conflict, intergroup dynamics, team building, managing technological and cultural change, etc. The programme designs were participative in that they encouraged participants to move between the "here and now" of interactive sessions and consideration of "back home" issues, but inevitably the participants' work concerns were forced into the pre-established framework of "topics" and the focus was on participants as individual learners. Little consideration was given in these programmes to any sustained exploration of the participants' work problems as part of a complex organizational reality shaped by wider system dynamics.

This retreat from the pedagogical challenge of starting with the phenomenal world of the individual manager was not just a consequence of my conceptual framework. It was reinforced by the corporate world's rapid embrace of the managerial competency movement, which introduced a new, improved list of academically researched topics (competencies) that reinforced the expert status of management academics and consultants. And, if I am not mistaken, this approach is still very much in evidence, at least in Australia. The topics may have changed (currently to include emotional intelligence, "breakthrough" culture change, transformative leadership, managing ambiguity, entrepreneurial mind-sets, strategic everything, etc.) but the programmes are still "rolled out" (a telling metaphor) and the ubiquity of the MBA paradigm (Newton, 1999a) seems to reinforce and to sanction this formulaic approach to management development. Of course, there is a place for formulas, when inputs can be controlled and standard outputs are required, but over the past few decades managers have had to deal increasingly with circumstances that are less predictable and less controllable. Gradually, this fact was brought home to me during the programmes I designed and conducted as more and more participants sought to speak with me during the breaks, wanting to discuss what worried them in their day to day work lives; the worries that did not easily fit the assumptions and format of this approach to management development.

Initially, I had been satisfied when the programme evaluations and follow-up revealed that individual participants had gained sufficient skill development to satisfy them and our respective corporate sponsors. However, another pattern in the evaluation data soon became apparent. Participants indicated that they often valued most the indirect learning gained through their interaction and dialogue with colleagues from other parts of their wider work system. I was curious about the ranking given to this aspect of the programmes, but I found it difficult to interest my corporate clients in pondering this evidence. And, I have to admit, it was easy to accept payment and not question too keenly the possible threats this posed to my primacy as the consultant. The demand for solution-driven consultancy continued to grow, along with the urgency for large-scale organizational change, and a strong focus developed on dealing with "resistance" in the implementation of change. It was as if the struggle of individual managers, working within their various roles, had little to offer organizations about the reality of their substantive work within a shifting environment. The focus remained on the individual *per se* as the fashion for downsizing began to take hold, further reducing curiosity about system dynamics among the survivors, while promoting a new demand for outplacement services from consultants. Ironically, this downsizing trend also produced a huge increase in demand from mature students for university qualifications in management. Some of these students wanted formal qualifications as a hoped-for protection against redundancy, while others genuinely wanted to understand what was happening to them and their organizations as the "new order" began to unfold (Newton, 1999b). As a management educator and consultant, I was perplexed about the efficacy of my work even as demand for my services escalated.

During this period I took some time out for my own professional development when I spent a year in the education faculty of the University of Massachusetts. This faculty embraced an ethos of "freedom to learn" and students were supported to negotiate a curriculum that was meaningful for their own career development. An opportunity I took was to participate in two conferences offered by the A. K. Rice Institute (Boston), in the tradition of the Learning for Leadership conferences developed by the Tavistock Institute of Human Relations (Miller, 1990). The intensity of this sort of experiential learning has been well documented (see Borwick, and Reed & Bazalgette, this volume), as has the evolving conceptualization of the "group relations" design (Miller, 1990). Suffice to say, my first exposure to this educational method enabled me to feel strongly, and gradually to understand, just how powerful can be the unconscious motivation in an organizational setting to use others as a means of shoring up a familiar role for oneself, even when this involves abandoning the work task and manipulating role relations so others can carry your uncertainty, doubts, and anxiety (Shapiro & Carr, 1991).

This deliberately promoted access to the unconscious dimension of organizational dynamics connected immediately with my previous experience as a management educator and consultant. It spoke to the worries and stress that my students and clients presented; worries that could never quite be categorized as neat problems to be solved. Subsequently, I began to study the conceptual basis of the group relations tradition and to experiment with ways of using its methods within my practice as a management educator. My aim was to devise an educational design that would enable and support students to explore the unconscious dynamics of their work role performance. This quest led me through the established works of Klein (1975), Bion (1961, 1962), Menzies-Lyth (1988), Miller and Rice (1967), and to later contributors such as Hirschhorn (1988). At the same time, I was intrigued by the educational challenge presented by Freire (1968) with his powerful evocation of the concept of "praxis": understanding and changing systems through the oscillating processes of taking action and questioning the systemic constraints on that action.

I began to realize that the postgraduate programme in which I taught offered a wonderful opportunity to seek collaboration with colleagues and students (the latter enrolled in part-time studies for between two and four years) to evolve a new way of learning to engage with and manage organization dynamics. The challenge was to develop, within a business school culture, an educational praxis that invited students to work with the raw experience of their work lives as they struggled to disentangle the fantasies of management qualifications from the reality of managerial practice. My colleague Susan Long has published a fuller account of this development (2004), but here I want to focus on one course I shaped within the programme. I called this course "Managing Oneself in Role", taking the title directly from Lawrence's (1979) chapter: "A concept for today: managing oneself in role". That chapter, appropriately, offered no prescription for how to manage oneself in role but it presented a compelling argument for each of us to take up the authority and responsibility to negotiate our roles in this world, and hence the ways in which our roles are related. Lawrence argued that in an increasingly complex, interconnected and turbulent environment, managing oneself in role is the essence of management, since it is pointless to depend on anyone else, be they a more senior manager or consultant, to provide the answers to our problems of relatedness through task.

Later, I discovered that Gordon Lawrence, too, had been greatly impressed by the work of Friere (personal communication), and as I met more people who had been influenced by, and who had helped to shape, the Tavistock tradition I found that a variety of approaches have evolved to working with organizational role dynamics. The contributors to this volume amply illustrate that evolution, and this chapter describes one form of organizational role analysis that I developed within a university context.

The aim of the university course titled "Managing Oneself in Role" is simple yet demanding. The aim is to provoke and to assist students into a deeper than usual understanding of how individual psychodynamic patterns may connect with work system dynamics, thus creating the force field that shapes a "given" work role. [See Krantz & Maltz (1997) for elaboration of the idea of a role as both "given" and "taken".] This deeper understanding may then be used to seek optimal alignment between the boundaries of a work role, the task from which it is derived, and the authority of the role holder. Students work towards this aim primarily by performing the task of helping a client achieve such understanding for him/herself. They come to this course in the fourth semester of their part-time programme, having already studied system psychodynamic theory and participated in experiential learning events similar to those in the Learning for Leadership tradition. Within the course they are required to take up the role of consultant to a self-selected client who is seeking assistance to better understand and perform their work role. In this sense, the course has a double educational task (Bridger, 1990) of (i) helping students learn what they have absorbed already about organization dynamics through the challenge of using their internalized knowledge and experience to assist another person (client), and (ii) through the reflective space of the course discovering more about their own unconscious dynamics in the challenge of taking up the role of consultant. Gradually, through the exploration of relevant concepts, practicum sessions, and peer-group reflection within class time, students come, for example, to realize the "role idea" (Reed, 1976) that shapes their way of being a consultant in this process, at the same time as they are helping their client to discover the role idea that shapes his/her work practice.

The structure of the course is typically of two-hour classes spread over fourteen weeks.

Weeks one to four are devoted to analysing selected readings (such as those in the appended bibliography and in this volume), discussing the aim and possible methods for a role consultation, and identification of tensions these students currently experience in their own work roles. The latter exercise forms a basis for reminding each other of the consultation's focus as person-in-role, not individual personality (see Borwick, and Reed & Bazalgette this volume).

Weeks five to six involve a practicum/demonstration of some kind. This may involve staff or invited "professionals", working with volunteer students or "guest" managers as clients, demonstrating in class how they negotiate a role consultation and begin the collaborative work of discovering how the client has come to construe their work role to him/herself, while gradually revealing the constellation of intrapsychic, group, and task-related forces that permeate the client's work role experience. The demonstrator may also share some of their experience in performing this sort of work, including its pitfalls, and reflect on how they have crafted their own style. Time may also be taken to explore different techniques that can be used, such as work drawings and work role biographies (Gould, 1987; Sievers & Beumer, and Long, this volume).

The message is reinforced that within the essential constraints of keeping the consultation focused on the "task" of examining collaboratively the client's chosen work role, and providing appropriate containment through reliable boundaries of time, space, and attention, each student must discover how to bring their own knowledge, skill, and experience into the role of consultant.

The practicum also raises issues of ethics: for instance, concerns for maintaining appropriate confidentiality when this sort of consultation is sponsored by an employer; and of providing anonymity and confidentiality for clients within the academic context. The latter includes negotiating the use of client material in the student's written assignment. Students are advised not to offer their client a copy of their written assignment but rather to encourage the client to develop his/her own reflective paper. The aim of this stance is to preserve the "freedom to learn" as a central aspect of the student role, and to encourage the client's responsibility for their own reflective practice. What agreements students actually enter into under the initial pressure of the task often provides much grist for learning and sometimes necessitates collaborative renegotiation with the client.

In weeks six to eleven students have the responsibility for finding a volunteer client who is experiencing difficulty in performing his/her work role and who is willing to undertake a role consultation involving four or five sessions, each of ninety minutes duration. These are the suggested parameters within the constraints of the programme and may be varied by the students in some cases.

During these weeks the class time is devoted to supervision of the students' progress in conducting their role consultations. This supervision may be offered within the whole group, depending upon the number of students, or in sub-groups, with each student given time to tell the unfolding story of the consultation with their client as their peers listen supportively and, as appropriate, offer their own reactions, associations, and thoughts. The role of the staff member is important in this process as someone who can support students in thinking together about the unconscious communication that may be occurring between consultant and client. Such unconscious communication may be revealed in difficulties the consultant has in staying on task, of maintaining agreed boundaries, of leading a balanced consideration of the client's material, and in attending to the emotional dimension of the consultation, or lack thereof.

The creation of this sort of reflective space (French, 1997) within the classroom has proved vital to the likelihood of students developing insight to the unconscious forces that systemically shape the client's work role. Supportive consideration of how the student consultant may be internalizing and/or enacting unconscious content, and how he/she may frame a working hypothesis (Lawrence, 1999; Reed & Bazalgette, this volume) for testing with the client, is essential to this form of Organizational Role Analysis. It also underpins any coaching the consultant may provide to strengthen the client's own capacities for "managing oneself in role".

Two brief examples from the course illustrate this possibility:

Example one

The student consultant, a senior manager in a professional services firm, had negotiated with his client, an upper level manager in a government department, to conduct the five agreed sessions of role consultation at a picnic table in a public park, before business hours. Members of the reflection group were incredulous at this arrangement. It seemed so at odds both with this group's understanding of role consultation as a professional development activity and with their image of the student consultant's usual professional practice.

The student admitted that it was not the sort of arrangement he had envisaged either, and he felt acutely self-conscious about it, yet he defended stoutly his acceptance of the client's claim to not being available at any other time or place. An early association to this material by a member of the reflection group was of two undercover agents having clandestine meetings in a deserted park. This image found considerable resonance in the group and was readily remembered in subsequent sessions.

After two meetings with his client, the student consultant revealed his growing state of bewilderment and frustration that the consultation was not "going anywhere", and members of the reflection group reported feelings of "voyeurism" and "eavesdropping" as they listened each week to a story that told of this client/manager's preoccupation with power politics between he and his colleagues, "off the record" sexual liaisons within the workplace, and extreme concern for his career ambitions. The data was titillating, but no one knew what to do with it, least of all the student consultant who was feeling embarrassingly inept and regretting the "picnic table" arrangements he had agreed to.

The tendency to blame a "bad" client and inadequate arrangements was acknowledged, and resisted, as the student consultant and supervision group endured awkward periods of feeling stuck. Then, one member of the group offered the reflection that she had heard a lot of lurid information about what this client thought, felt, and did during his time at work, but now realized she had no idea what this manager was actually paid to do. This observation startled everyone. Then slowly it dawned on the student consultant (and the reflection group) that so far he had not even thought to ask his client what he was actually supposed to be doing in his work role. The student consultant had been so swept away by the undertow of his client's political immersion, reflected so well in the "clandestine" consultation arrangements and enacted in his inability to keep his mind on the task of the consultation, that he had forgotten the fundamentals. Most importantly, with the help of the reflective space of the class group, he could now grasp the client's unconscious communication of how pervasive and invasive was the political culture surrounding his work role. The student consultant, steadied by his growing understanding of how he had been seduced into a particular enactment of power-based relationships, could begin to recover his authority to direct attention to the work task and, in the process, help his client to do the same.

Example two

This student negotiated to conduct an Organizational Role Analysis with a shift supervisor from the ambulance service. After the first consultation session with her female client, she came to the class reflection group feeling very nervous about revealing her experience of the encounter. She was worried what the group would think of her when she described her personal reactions. The group took some time to reassure each other that they would strive to view her data as an aspect of the work and not just as a personal idiosyncracy. Encouraged, the student consultant reported that she had experienced, for some unknown reason, a level of intimacy in the presence of her client that was almost unbearable. She described herself as feeling "psychologically—in a state of undress". This included being acutely conscious of some skin blemishes on her face and of trying to sit in a way that hid these from the client, who, for her part seemed to be arranging things so they sat as close as possible; even leaning over the consultant as she showed her a work report.

The reflection group listened supportively to this obviously unnerving experience but could not make much of it. The consultation continued and each week the student consultant reported on the data she was gathering about the work of ambulance officers and what it felt like for her client to be the female supervisor of this male workforce. Gradually a link was forming in her mind between her initial emotional reactions and what her client had told her about the distress ambulance officers often had to deal with. For instance, they often found the relatives and friends of a patient in states of emotional disintegration and physical undress when they first arrived at the scene of an emergency.

The student consultant formulated a working hypothesis that her experience at that first meeting was part of an unconscious communication from her client about the unacknowledged emotional labour in her supervisory role. When she took this working hypothesis back to her client it led to a revealing analysis of the way in which the client and her staff used detailed, written work reports to close off each assignment without ever discussing the emotional impact of what they had just experienced. The client was able then to reflect on how she and the ambulance officers were using the reports defensively, while at the same time becoming obsessed with occupational health and safety issues. They were spending more and more time compiling detailed written reports of their work, as a basis for stress-related sick leave claims, rather than attend to the emotional distress within the work, as an aspect of managing themselves within role. Subsequently, the client became open to a more profound sense of what managing might mean from within her work role and the student group, among other things, learned that emotions felt personally might actually derive from the work system, and that this possibility could be explored between two role holders by means of a working hypothesis.

Postscript

An unanticipated but rewarding outcome of this assignment for both student and staff, was that the executive to whom this student reported in her own work organization became so impressed at her growing ability to "work in the 'grey zone', when everyone else is looking for black or white", that he too became a student in the programme.

Weeks twelve to fourteen of the course are given to students' reflections on how they concluded their consultations, what links they can make between the way they took up the role of consultant and the way in which they take up their own work roles. Their experience within the course provides a powerful opportunity to discover patterns in their own personal authority (Gould, 1993) and the support to continue their struggle to disentangle what they bring to their work roles and what the organizational system projects into them. For instance, the degree of personal authority they take up to explore and negotiate the boundaries of a role within a particular system. Or, how they manage the tensions between personal relationships and role relatedness within their work (see Reed & Bazalgette, this volume).

Inevitably, some of the clients of these students seem to gain more than others from their consultation, so the students' various feelings of "success" and "failure" are examined to discern the presence or absence of negotiated arrangements and capacities for containing the client's experience and for encouraging a collaborative analysis of the data. This review assists students to shape their formal written assignment, which takes the form of a reflective report, specifying the critical steps in the consultation and explaining how the consultant used his/her own experience and grasp of relevant concepts to work with the client, whether successfully or not. Some students become enthused at the prospect of undertaking further training in role consultation, grasping its possibilities

for in-depth coaching, while other students are content with how
the experience has challenged their capacities to work in role and
to understand more about the unconscious processes that may pull
them out of role, and off task. As one student wrote about his most
significant learning: "That how I am in role is so clearly a product
of the model I have in mind for that role. I have discovered that the
difficulty of the work is 'really' the point—to notice that and to
work with it."

Conclusion

As the efficacy of traditional approaches to management education
is increasingly called into question (Gosling & Mintzberg, 2003), the
interest in individual coaching is rising dramatically. Quite possibly
this interest in coaching will be another passing fad, particularly if
it turns out to be only a disguised attempt to change managers as
individuals and gets represented in business schools as another
topic to be added to the curriculum. This chapter has outlined an
alternative approach that brings the difficulty of managing oneself
in role directly into the classroom. It requires the student manager
to engage directly with dynamics of a person-in-role-in-a-system,
and it supports a reflective exploration of the system psychodynamics that permeate that engagement. Rather than view coaching
as an end in itself, I contend that by placing a process of learning
about role consultation within the appropriately bounded space of
a university programme, students of management have the opportunity to not only discover their own capacities for *coaching-in-
depth*, but also strengthen their capacities for *managing oneself in role*.

Concluding comments.
Organizational Role Analysis:
from here to where?

Susan Long, John Newton, and Burkard Sievers

E xecutive Coaching is a growing field. Many executives seek out coaches to improve their skills and personal capacities. Companies often seek coaches for senior staff to improve their role perfomance and hence benefit the company overall. But most coaching is focused on the individual and their performance, as the name derived from sports coaching implies. Even when a team approach is taken, the emphasis is upon individual performers, or at most on the team as a group of interacting individual personalities. For example, the International Coach Federation (2004) has the following on its website:

> Professional coaches provide an ongoing partnership designed to help clients produce fulfilling results in their personal and professional lives. Coaches help people improve their performances and enhance the quality of their lives. Coaches are trained to listen, to observe and to customize their approach to individual client needs. They seek to elicit solutions and strategies from the client; they believe the client is naturally creative and resourceful. The coach's job is to provide support to enhance the skills, resources, and creativity that the client already has.

Organizational role analysis, as described in this volume, emphasizes the ideas of system and role in contradistinction to character and personality. It is the place of the role in the overall system that is explored—both in the mind of role holders and the mind of the outside observer. Beyond coaching as described by the Coach Federation, ORA places focus on the system as well as the person. For example,

> ORA provides a professional context for leaders and managers of institutions
>
> • to examine and articulate their current working experience
> • to analyse it in its organisational setting to sharpen up the meaning of that experience in terms of purpose, systems and boundaries
> • to grasp opportunities to find, make and take up their organisational roles more effectively
> • to transform their contribution towards achieving the corporate aims of their institution. [Grubb Institute Website, 2004]

Borwick, for instance, points out how this emphasis on system is critical to change in organizations where roles are held specifically within time limits to get a job done, rather than held in perpetuity as are family roles. When a role is taken up specifically for an organizational task rather than as a social inheritance it is potentially easier for individual role holders, in their minds, to separate the needs and demands of the role from their own personal characterisitics and abilities in taking up that role. So too, is it easier to understand the needs and demands of other roles and to see these apart from the personal characteristics of other role holders in those roles. Both person and role are important, but the distinction between the two is critical because it allows the role holder to understand his or her part in the system as something beyond self or ego. This shift in perspective, described by Lawrence (following Bion) as the shift from Oedipus to Sphinx is a crucial element in role analysis work. It is critical theoretically because of the fidelity to a systems emphasis. It is critical methodologically because it facilitates change in role development and role performance. Within this perspective, the role holder is free to use working hypotheses about role without being caught in personal defences about self.

Here: the method as used

While the theory behind the ORA method has been elaborated in this volume, the concluding section here will place emphasis on method. There are three aspects of the method to be stressed: context, the use of working hypotheses, and collaborative effort. These have been severally discussed in the preceding chapters but a summary may be useful.

1.   The first is the importance of the *context*. This means that ORA has a focus on the system within which the roles examined are located. It is no simple thing to discover this system. Each role holder will have a different "system-in-the-mind" from which they operate. Moreover, the system will be in flux and change with different aspects coming to the fore at different times. This is so evident that to think there is a singular reality to any organizational system is futile.

    However, it is helpful to think of the organization as a complex system of multiple agreements including agreements about roles and tasks emerging from each role holder's "system (organiza-tion/institution)-in-the-mind" (Armstrong, 1991; Hutton, Bazelgette, & Reed, 1992) or "system-in-experience" (Long, Newton, & Dalgleish, 2000). Many of these agreements may be consciously decided. Many are unconsciously decided and enacted. To make things even more complex, each of these agreements has the potential to affect agreements elsewhere in the system. ORA has the task of exploring this system from the standpoint of the role holder(s) involved.

    In practice:

- When the ORA moves toward exploring the system (the system/organization-in-the-mind of the client) certain ques-tions arise. How does the system look from this role? What does the system demand of this role? What does the system "put into" this role through its structure and dynamics?
- When the ORA moves toward exploring the experience of the role holder other questions arise. What thoughts, motives and emotions are generated by the role? What skills and capacities does the person bring from their training, personality, and history? How is the role shaped by these?

- When looking across all three the ORA process highlights the effects on the system of how the person takes up and shapes and works with the authority of the role. Also seen is how the system shapes the role and fills the person so that they experience issues that are *in* them but not *of* them (to use Armstrong's evocative language). (From: "Notes for organisation role consultation", Susan Long, RMIT University, Melbourne, Australia.)

2. The exploration proceeds through the use of *working hypotheses*. As the role holder, the consultant or the group explore a work role, working hypotheses about the system emerge. These may be implicitly present in the questions raised for the exploration or they may be more deeply hidden or unconsciously present in the exploration. The ORA method requires that such implicit and hidden hypotheses are made explicit and hence can be explored and themselves questioned. The working hypothesis has the virtue of bringing forward the assumptions held by role holders about their systems in a way that is exploratory rather than personally threatening. Moreover, if the consultant has also to frame his or her questions and comments in the context of a working hypothesis, then the tendency to "advise" rather than work as a co-explorer with the role holder is diminished. This leads to the next point.

3. The ORA method is *collaborative*. The role holder and consultant or consulting group work together to discover the role and system. This is in contrast to a method where an "expert" advises a role holder on how he or she should be behaving or performing. Through the development of working hypotheses about the role and its system, the role holder is able to make decisions about how to proceed in role. One could say that authority for the ORA is evenly distributed.

   As part of this collaborative process, the temporary system of the role analysis is itself an important source of information. Exploration through working hypotheses about how the role analysis is proceeding, the dynamics within the sessions and the thoughts and feelings about the sessions may be helpful in understanding the wider system of the role being explored. This is because the role analysis sessions, through parallel process or projective identification themselves very often become a microcosm of the system under exploration. All parties within the ORA need to explore collaboratively what is emerging for them, in role, in order to develop working hypotheses that may be helpful to the client. This idea of collaborative work does not contradict but heightens the importance of professionalism in the consultant role.

Where: the further development of ORA

This volume has looked at the origins of Organizational Role Analysis and some of its further developments. This just begins to touch the subject. There are many applications that could follow. For example, while many consultants trained in this method use it with individual clients, there has been the potential from the beginning for its use with groups within organizations. The use of collaborative exploration, working hypotheses, and the emphasis on system and role make it a method highly suitable for organizational change and development. The editors know of examples where ORA has been used with managers and subordinates in a close exploration of the way their roles interact. The method provides a more far-reaching and in-depth approach than the often used 360 degrees exercise because of the emphasis on the system as well as the players. It could also be used with new teams to examine scenarios where future roles are envisaged.

In general, the coaching literature and the literature on ORA has neglected lifestage theory, as pointed out by Gould in this book. Increasingly, young people are taking up quite senior roles in organizations and the community, as are women and people from diverse backgrounds. No longer are senior leadership positions the sole right of age, maleness, or restricted cultural or socio-economic groups. In the future we should address issues where roles are being taken up by non-traditional role holders. How might role analysis best be conducted for this purpose? What might be the training required for those consultants engaging in role analysis or role consultation with a diverse range of clients?

Another major area of change is around the nature of organization, whether in the private, public, or community sectors. How might ORA take the workplace changes of the past ten years into account? For instance, what management education might be available to support, through evolving ORA methods, people working in organizations that are flattening structures, promoting knowledge networks and constantly calling for innovation while demanding an accountability reponsive to change? How might consultants integrate ORA methodology into their work when consulting to changing structures, cultures, and dynamics in organizations?

One issue that preoccupies coaches who are also trained psychologists, therapists, or counsellors is the difference between counselling, therapy, and coaching. For instance, this was a major theme at the conference of the Australian Psychological Association's Coaching Interest Group, July 2004. The distinction between coaching and therapy or counselling is an important one. Not least because therapy and counselling require highly specialized psychological training, whereas executive coaching requires specialized management and organizational knowledge. The two arenas may overlap, but the practice, task, and approach are different.

The ORA approach helps make the distinction clearer. While therapy tends to focus on the personality and individual skills, ORA focuses on the role within the system. This distinction is not absolute. There are therapies that place emphasis on the roles that people take up, for example, in the family system, and ORA does look at the skills, abilities, and capacities that the role holder brings to the role. None the less, the emphasis and focus is different. The distinction is drawn mainly through the task involved. ORA has the primary task of examining the role within its system, which includes how it is taken up by the role holder.

However, there is a continuing need for lively discussion and debate around the distinctions between ORA, coaching, mentoring, and counselling. Each has its distinct approaches, theories, and methods. The editors of this volume stress the need for intending practitioners to gain reputable training in the ORA method that includes undergoing a role analysis oneself as well as having access to supervised practice. The practice of ORA involves more than a simple translation of skills from other professional areas.

The increasing use of ORA as a coaching method does lead to the need for more research about its effectiveness. This might include research on outcomes and evaluation of the method in a variety of settings. Linked to this would be an examination of the ethical and philosophical implications of the use of the ORA method. Currently, those working with Organizational Role Analysis vouch for its effectiveness through personal experience. But it would be helpful to the intending practitioner if more research were conducted into those factors that increased its effectiveness and those occasions when outcomes were less positive.

REFERENCES

A. K. Rice Institute. www.akriceinstitute.org

Armstrong, D. (1991). The institution-in-the-mind: reflections on the relations of psycho-analysis to work with institutions. Paper presented at a conference: "Psycho-analysis and the Public Sphere", East London Polytechnic.

Armstrong, D. (1995). The analytic object in organizational work. Presented at the annual Symposium of the International Society for the Psychoanalytic Study of Organizations, London.

Armstrong, D. (1997). The "institution-in-the-mind". Reflections on the relation of psychoanalysis to work with institutions. *Free Associations*, 7(41): 1–14.

Armstrong, D. G. (1997). The "Institution-in-the-mind": reflections on the relevance of psychoanalysis to work with institutions. *Free Associations*, 7(1) (No.41): 1–14.

Aronson, J. K. (1996). The use of the telephone as a transitional space in the treatment of a severely masochistic anorexic patient. In: J. Edward & J. Sanville (Eds.), *Fostering Healing and Growth: A Psychoanalytic Social Work Approach* (pp. 163–178). Northvale, NJ: Jason Aronson.

Auer-Hunzinger, V., & Sievers, B. (1991). Organisatorische Rollen-analyse und-beratung. Ein Beitrag zur Aktionsforschung. *Gruppendynamik*, 22: 33–46.

Bateson, G. (1972). *Steps to an Ecology of Mind.* New York: Chandler.

Beumer, U. (1998). "Schläft ein Lied in allen Dingen . . .". Dingliche Objekte und räumliche Szenarien in der psychoanalytischen Organizationssupervision. *Freie Assoziation, 1:* 277–303

Bion W. R. (1961). *Experiences in Groups.* London: Tavistock.

Bion, W. R. (1962). *Learning from Experience.* London: Heinemann.

Bion W. R. (1963). *Elements of Psychoanalysis.* London: Maresfield Reprints.

Bion, W. R. (1965). *Transformations.* London: Karnac, 1984.

Bion, W. R. (1970). Container and contained. In: *Attention and Interpretation* (pp. 72–83). London: Maresfield Reprints.

Biran, H. (2003). The difficulty of transforming terror into dialogue. *Group Analysis, 36*(4): 490–502.

Bollas, C. (1987). *The Shadow of the Object. Psychoanalysis of the Unthought Known.* London: Free Association Books.

Bollas, C. (1992). *Being a Character. Psychoanalysis and Self Experience.* New York: Hill & Wang.

Borwick, I. (1997). *Group Strategy and Action Program.* New York: Borwick International.

Bridger, H. (1990). Course and working conferences as transitional learning institutions. In: E. Trist & H. Murray (Eds.), *The Social Engagement of Social Science. A Tavistock Anthology. Volume 1: The Socio-Psychological Approach.* London: Free Association Books.

Brunning, H. (2001). The six domains of executive coaching. *Organizational and Social Dynamics, 2:* 254–263.

Capra, F. (1997). *The Web of Life.* London: Flamingo.

Capra, F. (2003). *The Hidden Connections.* London: Flamingo.

Carr, W. (1999). Can we speak of spirituality in institutions? In: J. F. Cobble & C. M Elliott (Eds.), *The Hidden Spirit* (pp. 109–117). Matthews, NC: CMR Press.

Chapman, J. (1999). Hatred and corruption of task. *Socio-Analysis. The Journal of the Australian Institute of Socio-Analysis, 1*(2): pp. 127–150.

Civin, M. (2000). *Male, Female, Email: The Struggle for Relatedness in a Paranoid Society.* New York: Other Press.

Erikson, E. H. (1985). *The Life Cycle Completed.* New York: W. Norton.

Fitzgerald, C. (2002). Understanding and supporting development of executives at midlife. In: C. Fitzgerald & J. Garvey Berger (Eds.), *Executive Coaching: Practices and Perspectives.* Palo Alto, CA: Davies-Black Publications.

French, R. (1997). The teacher as container of anxiety: psychoanalysis and the role of the teacher. *Journal of Management Education, 21*: 483–495.

Freud, S. (1914). On narcissism: an introduction. *S.E., 14*: pp. 93–97. London: Hogarth.

Friere, P. (1968). *Pedagogy of the Oppressed.* New York: Herder and Herder.

Gosling, J., & Mintzberg, H. (2003). The five minds of a manager. *Harvard Business Review.* November: 54–63.

Gould, L. J. (1987). A methodology for assessing internal working models of the organization: applications to management and organizational development programs. Paper presented at the Symposium of the International Society for the Psychoanalytic Study of Organizations, October 24–25, New York City.

Gould, L. J. (1993). Contemporary perspectives on personal and organizational authority: the self in a system of work relationships. In: L. Hirschhorn & C. K. Barnett (Eds.), *The Psychodynamics of Organizations.* Philadelphia: Temple University Press.

Gould, L. J. (1999). A political visionary in mid-life: notes on leadership and the life cycle. In: R. French & R. Vince (Eds.), *Group Relations, Management and Organization* (pp. 17–86). Oxford: Oxford University Press.

Gould, L. J., Stein, M., & Stapley, L. (Eds.) (2001). *The Systems Psychodynamics of Organizations. Integrating the Group Relations Approach, Psychoanalytic and Open Systems Perspectives.* London: Karnac.

Gutmann, D. (1989). The decline of traditional defences against anxiety. In: *Proceedings of the First International Symposium on Group Relations, Keble College Oxford.* Washington, DC: A. K. Rice Institute.

Haubl, R. (1999). Die Hermeneutik des Szenischen in der Einzel- und Gruppenanalyse. *Gruppenpsychotherapie und Gruppendynamik, 35*: 17–53.

Hirschhorn, L. (1988). *The Workplace Within.* Cambridge, MA: MIT Press.

Hollway, W., & Jefferson, T. (2000). *Doing Qualitative Research Differently: Free Association, Narrative and the Interview Method.* London: Sage.

Hondrich, K. O. (1997). Latente und manifeste Sozialiät. Anregungen aus der Psychoanalyse für eine Sozioanalyse. In: P. Kutter (Ed.), Psychoanalyse Interdisziplinär (pp. 69–95). Frankfurt: Suhrkamp.

Hutton, J. (1997). Re-imagining the organization of an institution. In: E. Smith (Ed.), *Integrity and Change: Mental Health in the Marketplace*. London: Routledge.

Hutton, J., Bazalgette, J., & Armstrong, D. (1994). What does management really mean? In: R. Casemore, G. Dyos, A. Eden, K. Kellner, J. McAuley, & S. Moss (Eds.), *What Makes Consultancy Work— Understanding the Dynamics* (pp. 185–203). London: South Bank University Press.

Hutton, J., Bazalgette, J., & Reed, B. (1997). Organization-in-the-mind: a tool for leadership and management of institutions. In: J. E. Neumann, K. Kellner, & A. Dawson-Shepherd (Eds.), *Developing Organizational Consultancy* (pp. 113–126). London: Routledge.

Jung, C. G. (1971). The stages of life. In: J. Campbell (Ed.), *The Portable Jung*. New York: Viking Portable Library.

Karp, D. A. (1988). A decade of reminders: changing age consciousness between fifty and sixty years old. *The Gerontologist, 28*: 727–738.

Kirk, P. (2003). Voice and leadership: achieving distributed leadership through organizational role leadership and organizational conversation. Bristol Business School Research Paper, UK (submitted for publication).

Klein, M. (1963). *Our Adult World and its Roots in Infancy*. London: Heinemann.

Klein, M. (1975). *Envy and Gratitude and Other works 1946–1963*. London: Virago.

Kolb, D. (1984). *Experiential Learning: Experience as the Source of Learning and Development*. Englewood Cliffs, NJ: Prentice Hall.

König, K. (1986). *Angst und Persönlichkeit. Das Konzept vom steuernden Objekt und seine Anwendungen*. Göttingen: Vandenhoek & Rupprecht.

Krantz, J., & Maltz, M. (1997). A framework for consulting to organizational role. *Consulting Psychology Journal: Practice and Research, 49*(2): 137–151.

Larkin, L. (2000). Therapy without the person in the room. Presented at American Psychological Association Convention on Psychoanalysis and Psychotherapy in a Global Society, as part of a symposium: "Talking cure in the 21st century—telephone psychoanalysis". Washington, DC.

Lawrence, W. G. (1979). A concept for today: the management of oneself in role. In: W. G. Lawrence (Ed.), *Exploring Individual and Organizational Boundaries. A Tavistock Open Systems Approach* (pp. 235–249). Chichester. Wiley & Sons [reprinted London: Karnac, 1999].

Lawrence, W. G. (1979). *Exploring Individual and Organizational Boundaries*. Chichester: John Wiley & Sons.

Lawrence, W. G. (1985). Beyond the frames. In: M. Pines (Ed.), *Bion and Group Psychotherapy*. London: Routledge & Kegan Paul.

Lawrence, W. G. (1999). Centering of the Sphinx for the psychoanalytic study of organizations. *Socio-Analysis. Journal of the Australian Institute of Socio-Analysis*, 1(2): 99–126.

Lawrence, W. G. (2000). Thinking refracted. In: *Tongued with Fire. Groups in Experience* (pp. 1–30). London: Karnac.

Lawrence, W. G. (2003a). *Experiences in Social Dreaming*. London: Karnac.

Lawrence, W. G. (2003b). Narcissism vs. social-ism governing thinking in social systems. In: R. M. Lipgar & M. Pines (Eds.), *Building on Bion: Branches* (pp. 204–222). London: Jessica Kingsley.

Lawrence, W. G. (this volume)

Levinson, D. J. (1996). *Seasons of a Woman's Life*. New York: Alfred A. Knopf.

Levinson, D. J., Darrow, C. N., Klein, E. B., Levinson, M. H., & McKee, B. (1978.) *Seasons of a Man's Life*. New York: Alfred A. Knopf.

Long, S. (1999). Who am I at work? An exploration of work identifications and identity. *Socio-Analysis*, 1: 48–64

Long, S. (2000). The internal team: a discussion of the socio-emotional dynamics of team (work). Paper presented at The International Society for the Psychoanalytic Study of Organizations Symposium, London. http://www.sba.oakland.edu/ispso/html./2000Symposium/Long2000.htm

Long, S. (2004). Developing an institution for experiential learning. In: L. J. Gould, L. F. Stapley, & M. Stein (Eds.), *Experiential Learning in Organizations. Applications of the Tavistock Group Relations Approach*. London: Karnac.

Long, S., Newton, J., & Dalgleish, J. (2000). In the presence of the other: developing working relations for organizational learning. In: E. Klein, F Gablenick, & P. Herr (Eds.), *Dynamic Consultation in a Changing Workplace*. Madison, CT: Psychosocial Press.

Manosevitz, M. (2000). Telephone psychoanalysis: talking about bodily states in the absence of visual clues. Presented at American Psychological Association Convention on Psychoanalysis and Psychotherapy in a Global Society, as part of a symposium: "Talking cure in the 21st century—telephone psychoanalysis". Washington, DC.

Mant, A. (1976). How to analyse management. *Management Today*, October.

Menzies-Lyth, I. (1988). *Containing Anxiety in Institutions. Selected Essays*. London: Free Association Press.

Mersky, R. (2001). Falling from grace—when consultants go out of role: enactment in the service of organizational consultancy. *Socio-Analysis*, 3: 37–53.

Miller, E. J. (1990). Experiential learning in groups. 1. The development of the Leicester Model. In: E. Trist & H. Murray (Eds.), *The Social Engagement of Social Science. A Tavistock Anthology. Volume 1: The Socio-Psychological Approach* (pp. 165–185). London: Free Association.

Miller, E. J., & Rice, A. K. (1967). *Systems of Organisation: Task and Sentient Systems and their Boundary Control*. London: Tavistock.

Newton, J. F. (1999a). Clinging to the MBA syndicate: Shallowness and "second skin" learning in management education. *Socio-Analysis. The Journal of the Australian Institute of Socio-Analysis*, 1: 151–175.

Newton, J. F. (1999b). Learning from the experience in management education: a psychodynamic perspective. PhD thesis (unpublished): Monash University, Australia.

Obholzer, A. (1994). Managing anxieties in public sector organizations. In: A. Obholzer & V. Zagier Roberts (Eds.), *The Unconscious at Work: Individual and Organizational Stress in the Human Services*. London: Routledge.

Ohlmeier, D. (1976). Gruppeneigenschaften des psychischen Apparates. In: D. Eicke (Ed.), *Die Psychologie des 20. Jahrhunderts. Vol. II* (pp. 1133–1144). Zürich: Kindler.

Quine, C., & Hutton, J. (1992). Finding, making and taking the role of head: a Grubb Institute perspective on mentoring for headteachers. Unpublished manuscript of Grubb Institute, London.

Reed, B. D. (1976). Organizational Role Analysis. In: C. L. Cooper (Ed.), *Developing Social Skills in Managers. Advances in Group Training* (pp. 89–102). London: Macmillan.

Reed, B. D. (1978). *The Dynamics of Religion*. London: Darton, Longman and Todd.

Reed, B. D., Hutton, J., & Bazalgette, J. (2002). *Becoming Fit for Purpose: Christian Leadership of Failing Church of England Schools*. London: The Grubb Institute.

Reed, M, & Anthony, P. (1995). Professionalizing management and managing professionalization: British management in the 1980s. In: J. Holloway, J. Lewis, & G. Mallory (Eds.), *Performance Measurement and Evaluation*. London: Sage (in association with the The Open University).

Revans, R. (1983). *ABC of Action Learning*. United Kingdom: Chartwell Bratt.

Rice, A. K. (1963). *The Enterprise and its Environment*. London: Tavistock.

Rice, A. K. (1965). *Learning for Leadership*. London: Tavistock.

Rice, A. K. (1969). Individual, group and inter-group processes. *Human Relations*, 22: 565–584.

Rycroft, C. (1972). *A Critical Dictionary of Psychoanalysis*. Harmondsworth: Penguin.

Schein, E. (1993). On dialogue, culture, and organizational learning. *Organisational Dynamics*, 22(2): 40–52.

Shapiro, E., & Carr, W. (1991). *Lost in Familiar Places: Making New Connections Between Individual and Society*. New Haven, NJ: Yale University Press.

Sievers, B. (1991). Mitarbeiter sind keine Olympioniken. *Personalführung*, 4: 272–274.

Sievers, B. (1995a) Die Rolle des Managers. *Organizationsberatung—Supervision—Clinical Management*: 2(1): 63–72.

Sievers, B. (1995b). Characters in search of a theatre. Organization as theatre for the drama of childhood and the drama at work. *Free Associations*, 5(2) (No. 34): 196–220.

Sievers, B., & Beumer, U. (2005). Organizational Role Analysis and consultation: the organization as inner object. In: this volume.

Stierlin, H. (1971). Die Funktion innerer Objekte. *Psyche, 25*: 81–99.

Stolorow, R. D., Brandchaft, B., & Atwood, G. E. (1996). *Psychoanalytische Behandlung. Ein intersubjektiver Ansatz*. Frankfurt: Fischer TB.

Sulkowicz, K. J. (2000). Paper presented at panel discussion on "The impact of the Internet and telemedicine on psychoanalysis". The American Psychoanalytic Association, Midwinter Meetings, December 15.

Triest, J. (1999). The inner drama of role taking in an organization. In: R. French, & R. Vince (Eds.), *Group Relations, Management, and Organization* (pp. 209–223). Oxford: University Press

Voß, G. G. (1998). Die Entgrenzung von Arbeit und Arbeitskraft. Eine subjektorientierte Interpretation des Wandels der Arbeit. *Mitteilungen aus der Arbeitsmarkt- und Berufsforschung, 3*: 473–487.

Weigand, W., & Sievers, B. (1985). Rolle und Beratung in Organizationen. *Supervision, 7*: 41–61.

Weiß, R. (1991). Selbstmanagement als Rollenmanagement. In: M. Lewkowicz (Ed.), *Neues Denken in der sozialen Arbeit: Mehr Ökologie – mehr Markt – mehr Management*, (pp. 210–218). Freiburg: Lambertus.

White, K. P. (2001). Applying learning from experience: the intersection of psychoanalysis and organizational role consultation. In: L. J. Gould, L. F. Stapley, & M. Stein (Eds.), *The Systems Psychodynamics of Organizations* (pp. 18–43). New York: Karnac.

Zalusky, S. (1998). Telephone analysis: out of sight, but not out of mind. *Journal of the American Psychoanalytic Association*, 46(4): http://www.psychomedia.it/pm/telecomm/telephone/zalusky2.htm

BIBLIOGRAPHY

Compiled by Burkard Sievers

Armstrong, D. (1994). *The Unthought Known. A Dialogue about a Consultant's Experience in Organisational Role Analysis.* London: The Grubb Institute.

Armstrong, D. (1995). The analytic object in organisational work. Unpublished, but available from Tavistock Consultancy Service and Tavistock Centre Library.

Armstrong, D. (1997). The 'Institution-in-the-Mind'. Reflections on the Relation of Psychoanalysis to Work with Institutions. *Free Associations, 7*(41): 1–14 http://human-nature.com/hraj/mind.html

Auer-Hunzinger, V., & Sievers, B. (1991). Organisatorische Rollenanalyse und -beratung. Ein Beitrag zur Aktionsforschung. *Gruppendynamik, 22*: 33–46.

Barber, W. H. (1987). Role analysis group: integrating and applying workshop learning. In: W. B. Reddy & C. C. Henderson (Eds.), *Training Theory and Practice* (pp.179–184). Arlington, VA: NTL Institute and University Associates.

Berry, A., & Tate, D. (1988). Success in a new task—a role consultation. *Management Education and Development, 19*: 215–226.

Beumer, U., & Sievers, B. (2000). Einzelsupervision als Rollenberatung. Die Organisation als inneres Objekt. *Supervision, 3*: 10–17.

Beumer, U, & Sievers, B. (2001). Die Organisation als inneres Objekt - Einzelsupervision als Rollenberatung. In: B. Oberhoff & U. Beumer (Eds.), *Theorie und Praxis psychoanalytischer Supervision* (pp. 108–123). Münster: Edition Humanistische Psychologie, Votum.

Eck, C. D. (1990). Rollencoaching als Supervision. In: G. Fatzer & C. D. Eck (Eds.), *Supervision und Beratung: Ein Handbuch* (pp. 209-248). Cologne: Edition Humanistische Psychologie.

Fatzer, G. (1990), Rollencoaching als Supervision von Führungskräften. *Supervision*, 17: 42–49.

French, R., & Simpson, P. (1997). A systemic approach to organizational role and the management of change. In: F. A. Stowell, R. L. Ison, R. Armson, J. Holloway, S. Jackson, & S. McRobb (Eds.), *Systems for Sustainability: People, Organisations and Environments* (pp. 709–713). London: Plenum.

French, R. & Simpson, P. (1999). Organizational roles and the management of change: a systemic approach. In: Y. Gabriel (Ed.), *Organizations in Depth. The Psychoanalysis of Organizations* (pp. 99–102). London: Sage.

Gemmill, G., & Kraus, G. (1988). Dynamics of covert role analysis: small groups. *Small Group Behavior*, 19(3): 299–311.

Gould, L. J. (1989). The key to charismatic executive leadership—the organisational role analysis method. Manuscript.

Gould, L. J. (1993). Contemporary perspectives on personal and organizational authority: the self in a system of work relationships. In: L. Hirschhorn & C. K. Barnett (Eds.), *The Psychodynamics of Organizations* (pp. 49–63). Philadelphia: Temple University Press.

Hantschk, I. (1994). Rollenberatung. In: H. Pühl (Ed.), *Handbuch der Supervision 2* (pp. 162–172). Berlin: Edition Marhold.

Hirschhorn, L. (1985). The psychodynamics of taking the role. In: A. D. Colman, M. H. Geller (Eds.), *Group Relations Reader 2* (pp. 335–351). Washington, DC: A. K. Rice Institute.

Hutton, J. M. (1996). Re-imagining the organisation of the institution: management in human service institutions. In: E. Smith (Ed.), *Integrity and Change: Mental Health in the Marketplace* (pp. 66–82). London: Routledge.

Hutton, J., Bazalgette, J., & Reed, B. (1997). Organisation-in-the-Mind: a tool for leadership and management of institutions. In: J. E. Neumann, K. Kellner, & A. Dawson-Shepherd (Eds.), *Developing Organizational Consultancy* (pp. 113–126). London: Routledge.

Krantz, J., & Maltz, M (1997). A framework for consulting to organizational role. *Consulting Psychology Journal: Practice and Research, 49*(2): 137–158.

Lawrence, W. G. (1979). A concept for today: the management of oneself in role. In: W. G. Lawrence (Ed.), *Exploring Individual and Organizational Boundaries. A Tavistock Open Systems Approach* (pp. 235–249). Chichester: Wiley & Sons [reprinted London: Karnac, 1999].

Lawrence, W. G. (1998). Selbstmanagement-in-Rollen. Ein aktuelles Konzept. *Freie Assoziation 1*: 37–57.

Long, S. D. (1999). Who am I at work? An exploration of work identifications and identity. *Socio-Analysis, 1*: 48–64.

Long, S. D. (2001). Wer bin ich bei der Arbeit? Ein Beitrag zur Identifikation und Identität bei der Arbeit. *Freie Assoziation, 4*: 47–69.

Long, S., Newton, J., & Chapman, J. (1999). Working across the tensions: organisational role analysis with pairs from the same organisation. Presentation at the ISPSO Symposium, Toronto, Canada. http://www.sba.oakland.edu/ispso/html/1999Symposium/Long1999.htm

Newton, J., Long, S., & Sievers, B. (Eds.) (2005). *Coaching In-Depth: The Organizational Role Analysis Approach.* London: Karnac.

Lorenzen, Z. (1996). Female leadership: some personal and professional reflections. *Leadership & Organization Development Journal, 17*(6): 24–31.

Reed, B. (1976). Organizational Role Analysis. In: C. L. Cooper (Ed.), *Developing Social Skills in Managers* (pp. 89–102). London: Macmillan.

Reed, B. D. (1999). Organisational Transformation: concepts of person, system, boundary, role, authority and power. In: J. Nelson et al. (Eds.), *Leading, Managing, Ministering—Challenging Questions for Church and Society* (pp. 243–262). Norwich: Canterbury Press.

Reed, B. (2001). An exploration of role as used in the Grubb Institute. London: The Grubb Institute.

Sievers, B. (1992). Rollenanalyse und -beratung. In: K. Schadow, J. Gutman, & H.-P. Scherer (Eds.), *Jahrbuch Weiterbildung* (pp. 90–92). Düsseldorf: Handelsblatt.

Sievers, B. (1993). Auf der Suche nach dem Theater. Organisationen als Theater für die Dramen der Kindheit und der Arbeit. *Gruppendynamik, 24*: 367–389.

Sievers, B. (1994). Towards a new myth of management. In: *Work, Death, and Life Itself. Essays on Management and Organization* (pp. 228–245). Berlin: de Gruyter.

Sievers, B. (1995). Characters in search of a theatre. Organization as theatre for the drama of childhood and the drama at work. *Free Associations, 5*(2) (No. 34): 196–220.

Sievers, B. (1995). Die Rolle des Managers. *Organisationsberatung--Supervision--Clinical Management, 2*(1): 63–72.

Simpson, P., & French, R. (1998). Managing oneself in role: a working tool for the management of change. *Public Money and Management, 18*(2): 45–50.

Triest, J. (1999). The inner drama of role taking in an organisation. In: R. French & R. Vince (Eds.), *Group Relations, Management, and Organization* (pp. 209–223). Oxford: Oxford: University Press.

Weigand, W., & Sievers, B. (1985). Rolle und Beratung in Organisationen. *Supervision, 7*: 41–61; *Organisationsentwicklung, 5*(3) (1986): 27–44; *GWG Zeitschrift, 18*(66) (1987): 9–16.

Weiß, R. (1991). Selbstmanagement als Rollenmanagement. In: M. Lewkowicz (Ed.), *Neues Denken in der sozialen Arbeit: Mehr Ökologie - mehr Markt - mehr Management* (pp. 210–218). Freiburg: Lambertus.

Weiß, R. (2000). Organisatorische Rollenberatung—Schnittstelle zwischen Organisationsentwicklung und Supervision. In: K. A. Geißler, v. L. Reinartz (Eds.), *Handbuch Personalentwicklung und Training* (pp. 1–17). Cologne: Verl.-Gruppe Dt. Wirtschaftsdienst 8.1.2.4.

White, K. P. (1996). Reflections from practice: the interface of psychoanalysis and organizational role consultation. Presentation at ISPSO Symposium, New York http://www.sba.oakland.edu/ispso/html/white.html

Related literature (a selection)

Diamond, M. A., & Allcorn, S. (1985). Psychological dimensions of role use in bureaucratic organizations. *Organizational Dynamics,* (Summer): 5–59.

Diamond, M. A., & Allcorn, S. (1986). Role formation as defensive activity in bureaucratic organizations. *Political Psychology, 7*: 709—732.

Flamholtz, E. G., & Randle, Y. (1987). *The Inner Game of Management. How to Make the Transition to a Managerial Role.* New York: AMACOM.

Graen, G. (1976). Role-making processes within complex organizations. In: M. P. Dunnette (Ed.), *Handbook of Industrial and Organizational Psychology* (pp. 1201–1245). Chicago: Rand-McNally.

Harrison, R. (1972). Role negotiation: a tough minded approach to team development. In: W. W. Burke & H. A. Hornstein (Eds.), *The Social Technology of Organization Development* (pp. 84–96). Fairfax, VA.: NTL Learning Resources Corp.

Harrison, R. (1977). Rollenverhandeln: Ein "harter" Ansatz zur Team-Entwicklung. In: B. Sievers (Ed.), *Organisationsentwicklung als Problem* (pp. 116–133). Stuttgart: Klett.

Hirschhorn, L. (1988). *The Workplace Within: Psychodynamics of Organizational Life*. Cambridge, MA.: MIT Press.

Hutton, J., Bazalgette, J., & Armstrong, D. (1994). What does management really mean? In: R. Casemore, G. Dyos, A. Eden, K. Kellner, J. McAuley, & S. Moss (Eds.), *What Makes Consultancy Work-- Understanding the Dynamics* (pp. 185–203). London: South Bank University Press.

Lawrence, W. G. (2000). Emotion in organizations: narcissism v. socialism. Paper presented at The International Society for the Psychoanalytic Study of Organizations 2000 Symposium, London. http://www.sba.oakland.edu/ispso/html/2000Symposium/Lawrence2000.htm

Lawrence, W. G. (2003). Narcissism v. social-ism governing thinking in social systems. In: R. M. Lipgar & M. Pines (Eds.), *Building on Bion: Branches* (pp. 204–222). London: Jessica Kingsley.

Long, S. (2000). The internal team: a discussion of the socio-emotional dynamics of team(work). Paper presented at The International Society for the Psychoanalytic Study of Organizations 2000 Symposium, London. http://www.sba.oakland.edu/ispso/html./2000Symposium/Long2000.htm

Long, S. D., & Newton, J. (1997). Educating the gut: socio-emotional aspects of the learning organization. *The Journal of Management Development, 16*(4): 284–301.

Miles, R. (1980). Organization boundary roles and units. In: J. F. Veiga & J. Yanouzas (Eds.), *The Dynamics of Organization Theory* (2nd edn. 1984). New York: West Publishing.

Miller, E. J. (1976). Introductory essay: role perspectives and the understanding of organizational behaviour. In: E. J. Miller (Ed.), *Task and Organization* (pp. 1–16). London: John Wiley & Sons.

Miller, E. J. (1990). Experiential learning in groups I: the development of the Leicester Model. In: E. L. Trist & H. Murray (Eds.), *The Social*

Engagement of Social Science. A Tavistock Anthology. Vol. I: The Socio-Psychological Perspective (pp. 165–185). London: Free Association.

Moxnes, P. (1999). Understanding roles: a psychodynamic model for role differentiation in groups. *Group Dynamics: Theory, Research, and Practice,* 3(2): 99–113.

Obholzer, A. (1989). Management and psychic reality. In: F. Gabelnick & A. W. Carr (Eds.), *Contributions to Social and Political Science. Proceedings of the First International Symposium on Group Relations.* Washington, DC: A. K. Rice Institute.

Orth, C. D., Wilkinson, H. E., & Benfari, R. C. (1987). The manager's role as coach and mentor. *Organizational Dynamics,* Spring: 66–74.

Paolillo, J. G. P. (1987). Role profiles for managers in different functional areas. *Group & Organization Studies,* 12(1): 109–118.

Reed, B., & Armstrong, D. (1988). *Professional Management. Notes prepared by The Grubb Institute on the Concepts Central to its Approach to Understanding How to Be a Manager.* London: The Grubb Institute.

Sandler, J. (1976). Gegenübertragung und Bereitschaft zur Rollenübernahme. *Psyche,* 4: 297–305.

Sievers, B. (1990). Nicht jede Organisation ist eine Kirche! Oder: Die Managementhierarchie beginnt ganz unten. *Supervision,* 17: 58–64.

Sievers, B. (1991), Mitarbeiter sind keine Olympioniken. *Personalführung,* 4: 272–274.

Sievers, B. (1994). AIDS in Selbsthilfeorganisationen. *Zeitschrift für Sexualforschung,* 7: 326–342.

Sievers, B. (2000). AIDS and the organization: a consultant's view of the coming plague. In: E. B. Klein, F. Gabelnick, & P. Herr (Eds.), *Dynamic Consultation in a Changing Workplace.* Madison, CT: Psychosocial Press.

Vickers, G. (1971). Institutional and Personal Roles. *Human Relations,* 24: 433–447.

West, M. A. (1987). Role innovation in the world of work. *British Journal of Social Psychology,* 26: 305–315.

INDEX